Christine Wilkinson

The Pivotal Role of Leisure Education: Finding Personal Fulfillment in This Century

The Pivotal Role of Leisure Education: Finding Personal Fulfillment in This Century

by Elie Cohen-Gewerc & Robert A. Stebbins

Venture Publishing, Inc.
State College, Pennsylvania

Production Manager: Richard Yocum
Manuscript Editing: George Lauer, Christina Manbeck

Library of Congress Catalogue Card Number 2007940629
ISBN-10: 1-892132-74-5
ISBN-13: 978-1-892132-74-1

Table of Contents

Chapter Six: Leisure and Lifelong Learning: Middle and Old Age...**91**

Introduction

Although it is presently true that the amounts of free time available to people in the West are not equally distributed, in general, there is more leisure time than ever before. However, for those who have it, a comparatively large amount of free time does not always result in leisure or in quality leisure. Boredom, which may occur in free time, is not leisure, and some leisure activities—even if they are not boring—are much less interesting, exciting, and personally enriching than they could be. Thus, a major challenge facing those who hope to better the lot of humankind, both Western and non-Western, is to find a way to acquaint people with the many interesting, exciting, and enriching leisure activities that are realistically available to them and to help those people define their own criteria for taking up some of the ones they find appealing.

For the authors, that way is leisure education, conceived of broadly as counselling, volunteering, and instructing in classrooms and elsewhere on such matters as the nature, types, and costs and rewards of various leisure activities possibly open to those receiving this kind of knowledge. From the authors' perspective, leisure education is a main way to enrich the lives of people who feel their leisure lifestyle is too uninteresting, unexciting, or incomplete, or perhaps even nonexistent. In other words, when it comes to improving the human condition, leisure education has a pivotal role to play in reaching that goal. Moreover, the time to pursue that goal is now, as the amount of free time is slowly expanding (for many people) and disenchantment with both modern work and unpleasant, nonwork obligations is growing at an even faster rate. That is, the twenty-first century belongs to leisure education.

Leisure education offers much to many. For example, through leisure education, people gain opportunities to explore new interests as well as often unknown aspects of themselves. The ancient philosophers focused mostly on work (with a little time set aside for writing on recreation), in an era largely dedicated to examining the needs of life in what was essentially a search for meaning as related to survival and to various practical concerns. By contrast, in this new century, people now feel a stirring of their own aspirations, undiluted by life's obligations. It is not enough simply to live in this new, open, and fertile world; we must be able to identify and realize new interests and learn how to realize these aspirations. Thus, leisure education must include a reconceptualization of such ideas as time, risk, freedom, adventure, socialization, uncertainty, and above all, education itself. In other words, education is much more than training people for work. Education introduces people to a more intimate encounter between self and life in its comprehensive sense.

The upshot of this is that education can no longer be regarded as limited to a period of fifteen or twenty years. Education must be conceived of more broadly as including lifelong learning. For example, leisure education becomes critical when we consider the growing allure of various leisure industries and the oftentimes weak market skills of consumers as they attempt to choose among them. This is a worldwide issue, however, unlike the aforementioned problem, where some people have so much free time that they need leisure education to help them use it for maximum benefit to self and community.

Our aim in this book is to weave together, on a world scale, the main strands of a manifesto on leisure education, aided by an international set of recognized experts in this field. Our principal audience consists of leisure educators themselves (as defined above), educators in general, researchers in the area, and leisure service providers, as well as students in leisure education and provision. Furthermore, educators of every stripe could conceivably be interested in what is said on these pages, as might some of the general public, whatever their age category. For it is in the general public where we find the "clients" of the leisure educator—the people who benefit from that expert's knowledge and experience.

Chapter One
The Idea of Leisure
by Elie Cohen-Gewerc and Robert A. Stebbins

Leisure is an everyday term whose etymological roots date to Roman times and the Latin noun *licere*. It later evolved into *leisir* in Old French and from there into leisure in Modern English, probably by way of the Norman Conquest of England in 1066 A.D., and into *le loisir* in Modern French. In everyday parlance, leisure refers both to the time left over after work and nonwork obligations—often called free time—and to the way we spend that time. Scientific attempts to define the idea have revolved, in considerable part, around the problems generated by this simplistic definition.

Scientifically speaking, leisure is uncoerced activity undertaken during free time. Uncoerced activity is positive activity that, using their abilities and resources, people both want to do and can do at either a personally satisfying or more fulfilling level (Stebbins 2005b). Note, in this regard, boredom occurring in free time is an uncoerced state, but it is also, decidedly, not something people want to experience. It is therefore not leisure; it is not positive experience, as just defined. Kaplan (1960:22-25) lists several other qualities of leisure that build on this basic definition. As uncoerced activity, leisure is the antithesis of work as an economic function. Moreover, it carries a pleasant expectation and recollection; involves a minimum of involuntary obligations; has a psychological perception of freedom; and offers a range of activity, ranging from inconsequence and insignificance to weightiness and importance.

Not all chapters in this book use the idea of leisure in ways consonant with this definition. Such variation is to be expected in matters as complex as leisure. The following section, in setting out the serious leisure perspective, demonstrates this complexity.

The Serious Leisure Perspective

The serious leisure perspective is a theoretical framework that synthesizes three main forms of leisure, showing, at once, their distinctive features, similarities, and interrelationships. Those forms are serious, casual, and project-based leisure. That the Perspective (wherever Perspective appears as shorthand for serious leisure perspective, to avoid confusion, the first letter will be capitalized) takes its name from the first of these features should, in no way, suggest that we regard it, in some abstract sense, as the most important or superior of the three. A book centered on the Perspective (Stebbins, 2006b) demonstrates the folly of that sort of thinking. Still, we will argue in this chapter that, on a specialized plane—in leisure education—serious leisure, compared with the other two, does occupy a special place.

Serious Leisure

Serious leisure is the systematic pursuit of an amateur, hobbyist, or volunteer activity that participants find so substantial, interesting, and fulfilling that they launch themselves on a (leisure) career centered on acquiring and expressing its special skills, knowledge, and experience (Stebbins, 1992; 2001c). The term was coined by the second author (Stebbins, 1982) to express the way the people he interviewed and observed viewed the importance of these three kinds of activity in their everyday lives. The adjective "serious" (a word the respondents often used) embodies such qualities as earnestness, sincerity, importance, and carefulness, rather than gravity, solemnity, joylessness, distress, and anxiety. Although the second set of terms occasionally describes serious leisure events, they are uncharacteristic of them and fail to nullify, or, in many cases, even dilute, the overall fulfillment gained by the participants. The idea of "career" in this definition follows sociological tradition, where careers are seen as available in all substantial, complex roles, including those in leisure. Finally, as we shall see shortly, serious leisure is distinct from casual leisure and project-based leisure.

Amateurs are found in art, science, sport, and entertainment, where they are linked in a variety of ways with professional counterparts. The two can be distinguished descriptively in that the activity in question constitutes a livelihood for professionals but not amateurs. Furthermore, most professionals work full-time at the activity whereas amateurs pursue it part-time. The part-time professionals in art and entertainment complicate this picture; although they work part-time, their work is judged by other professionals and by the amateurs in terms of professional quality. Amateurs and professionals are locked in and therefore defined by a system of relations linking them and their publics—the professional-amateur-public system (discussed in more detail in Stebbins, 1979; 1992, chap. 3). Hobbyists lack this professional alter ego, suggesting that, historically, all amateurs were hobbyists before their fields professionalized. Both types are drawn to their leisure pursuits significantly more by self-interest than by altruism, whereas volunteers engage in activities requiring a more or less equal blend of these two motives.

Volunteers offer uncoerced help—either formally or informally—with little or no pay, and do so for the benefit of both other people (beyond the volunteer's family) and they themselves (Stebbins, 2004a). This conception of volunteering revolves, in significant part, around a central subjective motivational question: it must be determined whether volunteers feel they are engaging in an enjoyable (casual leisure), fulfilling (serious leisure), or enjoyable and fulfilling (project-based leisure) core activity that they have had the option to accept or reject on their own terms. A key element in the leisure conception of volunteering is the felt absence of moral coercion to do the volunteer activity, an element that, in "marginal volunteering" (Stebbins, 2001a) may be experienced in degrees, as more or less coercive. The reigning conception of volunteering in nonprofit sector research is not that of volunteering as leisure, but rather volunteering as unpaid work. The first—an economic conception—defines volunteering as the absence of payment as livelihood, whether in money or in kind. For the most part, this definition leaves unanswered the messy question of motivation so crucial to the second definition, which is a volitional conception.

Serious leisure is further defined by six distinctive qualities, qualities uniformly found among its amateurs, hobbyists, and volunteers. One is the occasional need to persevere. Participants who want to continue experiencing the same level of fulfillment in the activity have to meet certain challenges from time to time. Thus, musicians must practice assiduously to master difficult musical passages, baseball players must throw repeatedly to perfect favorite pitches, and volunteers must search their imaginations for new approaches with which to help children with reading problems. It happens in all three types of serious leisure that the deepest fulfillment sometimes comes at the end of the activity rather than during it, from sticking with it through thick and thin, and from conquering adversity.

Another quality distinguishing all three types of serious leisure is the opportunity to follow a (leisure) career in the endeavor, shaped by its own special contingencies, turning points, and stages of achievement and involvement: a career that, in some fields, notably certain arts and sports, may nevertheless include decline. Moreover, most, if not all, careers here owe their existence to a third quality: serious leisure participants make significant personal effort using their specially acquired knowledge, training, or skill and, indeed at times, all three. Careers for serious leisure participants unfold along lines of their efforts to achieve, for instance, a high level of showmanship, athletic prowess, or scientific knowledge, or to accumulate formative experiences in a volunteer role. Moreover the act of making these efforts is part of this sense of career, for we experience ourselves over and over again as we bring our acquired and inherited qualities into play in support of our pursuit of a serious leisure activity.

Serious leisure is further distinguished by numerous durable benefits, or tangible, salutary outcomes such activity offers its participants. They are self-actualization, self-enrichment, self-expression, regeneration or renewal of self, feelings of accomplishment, enhancement of self-image, social interaction and sense of belonging, and lasting physical products of the activity (e.g., a painting, scientific paper, or piece of furniture). A further benefit — self-gratification, or pure fun, which is by far the most evanescent benefit in this list — is also enjoyed by casual leisure participants. The possibility of realizing such benefits constitutes a powerful goal in serious leisure.

Fifth, serious leisure is distinguished by a unique ethos that emerges in connection with each expression of it. An ethos is the spirit of the community of serious leisure participants, as manifested in shared attitudes, practices, values, beliefs, goals, and so on. The social world of the participants is the organizational milieu in which the associated ethos — at bottom a cultural formation — is expressed (as attitudes, beliefs, values) or realized (as practices, goals). According to Unruh (1980) every social world has its characteristic groups, events, routines, practices, and organizations. It is held together, to an important degree, by semiformal, or mediated, communication. In other words, in the typical case, social worlds are neither heavily bureaucratized nor substantially organized through intense face-to-face interaction. Rather, communication is commonly mediated by newsletters, posted notices, telephone messages, mass mailings, radio and television announcements, and similar means.

The social world is a diffuse, amorphous entity to be sure, but nevertheless one of great importance in the impersonal, segmented life of the modern urban community. Its importance is further amplified by a parallel element of the special ethos, which is missing from Unruh's conception, namely that such worlds are also constituted of a rich subculture. One function of this subculture is to interrelate the many components of this diffuse and amorphous entity. In other words, there is associated with each social world a set of special norms, values, beliefs, styles, moral principles, performance standards, and similar shared representations.

The sixth quality springs from the presence of the other five distinctive qualities: participants in serious leisure tend to identify strongly with their chosen pursuits. In contrast, most casual leisure, although not usually humiliating or despicable, is nonetheless too fleeting, mundane, and commonplace to become the basis for a distinctive identity for most people.

Furthermore, certain rewards and costs come with pursuing a hobbyist, amateur, or volunteer activity. As the following list shows, the rewards are predominantly personal.

Personal Rewards

1. Personal enrichment (cherished experiences)
2. Self-actualization (developing skills, abilities, knowledge)
3. Self-expression (expressing skills, abilities, knowledge already developed)
4. Self-image (known to others as a particular kind of serious leisure participant)
5. Self-gratification (combination of superficial enjoyment and deep satisfaction)
6. Re-creation (regeneration) of oneself through serious leisure after a day's work
7. Financial return (from a serious leisure activity)

Social Rewards

8. Social attraction (associating with other serious leisure participants, with clients as a volunteer, participating in the social world of the activity)
9. Group accomplishment (group effort in accomplishing a serious leisure project; senses of helping, being needed, being altruistic)
10. Contribution to the maintenance and development of the group (including senses of helping, being needed, being altruistic in making the contribution)

Additionally a participant's leisure fulfillment has been found to stem from a constellation of particular rewards gained from a given activity, be it boxing, ice climbing, or offering dance lessons to the elderly. It should be noted that the term "fulfillment" is preferred, because it points to a fulfilling experience, or more precisely, to a set of chronological experiences leading to development to the fullest of a person's gifts and character, to development of that person's full potential, which is certainly both a reward and a benefit of serious leisure. "Satisfaction," the term most commonly used in this area, sometimes refers to a satisfying experience that is fun or enjoyable (also referred to as gratifying). In another sense this noun may refer to meeting or satisfying a need or want. In neither instance does satisfaction denote the preferred sense of fulfillment just presented (Stebbins, 2004c).

Furthermore, the rewards are not only fulfilling in themselves, but also fulfilling as counterweights to the costs encountered in the activity. That is, every serious leisure activity contains its own combination of tensions, dislikes, and disappointments which each participant must confront in some way. Tensions and dislikes develop within the activity or through its imperfect mesh with work, family, and other leisure interests. Put more precisely, the goal of gaining fulfillment in serious leisure is the drive to experience the rewards of a given leisure activity, such that its costs are seen by the participant as more or less insignificant by comparison. This is at once the meaning of the activity for the participant and that person's motivation for engaging in it. It is this motivational sense of the concept of reward that distinguishes it from the idea of durable benefit set out earlier, an idea that emphasizes outcomes rather than antecedent conditions. Nonetheless, the two ideas constitute two sides of the same social-psychological coin.

Casual Leisure

Casual leisure is an immediately intrinsically rewarding, relatively short-lived, pleasurable activity requiring little or no special training to enjoy it. It is fundamentally hedonic, pursued for its significant level of pure enjoyment, or pleasure. The term was coined by the author in the conceptual statement about serious leisure (Stebbins, 1982), which at the time, depicted its casual counterpart as all activity not classifiable as serious (project-based leisure has since been added as a third form; see next section). As a scientific concept, casual leisure languished in this residual status, until Stebbins (1997b; 2001b), belatedly recognizing its centrality and importance in leisure studies, sought to elaborate the idea as a sensitizing concept for exploratory research, as he had earlier for serious leisure (see also Rojek, 1997). It is considerably less substantial and offers no career of the sort found in serious leisure.

Its eight types include play (including dabbling), relaxation (e.g., sitting, napping, strolling), passive entertainment (e.g., watching TV, reading books, listening to recorded music), active entertainment (e.g., games of chance, party games), sociable conversation, sensory stimulation (e.g., having sex, eating, drinking), and casual volunteering (as opposed to serious leisure, or career volunteering). The last and newest type—pleasurable aerobic activity—refers to physical activities that require effort sufficient to cause marked increase in respiration and heart rate.

Here, "aerobic activity" is referred to in the broad sense, as all activity that calls for such effort, which includes the routines pursued collectively in (narrowly conceived of) aerobics classes and those pursued individually by way of televised or video programs of aerobics (Stebbins, 2004b). Yet, as with its passive and active cousins in entertainment, pleasurable aerobic activity is basically casual leisure. That is, to do such activity requires little more than minimal skill, knowledge, or experience. Examples include the game of the Hash House Harriers (a type of treasure hunt in the outdoors), kickball (described in The Economist, 2005, as a cross between soccer and baseball), and such children's games as hide-and-seek.

It is likely that people pursue the different types of casual leisure in combinations of two and three at least as often as they pursue them separately. For instance, every type can be relaxing, producing, in this fashion, play-relaxation, passive entertainment-relaxation, and so on. Various combinations of play and sensory stimulation are also possible, as in experimenting with drug use, sexual activity, and thrill seeking. Additionally, sociable conversation accompanies some sessions of sensory stimulation (e.g., recreational drug use, curiosity seeking, displays of beauty), as well as some sessions of relaxation and active and passive entertainment, although such conversation normally tends to be rather truncated in the latter two.

Notwithstanding its hedonic nature, casual leisure is by no means wholly frivolous, for some clear costs and benefits accrue from pursuing it. Moreover, in contrast to the evanescent, hedonic property of casual leisure itself, these costs and benefits are enduring. The benefits include serendipitous creativity and discovery in play, regeneration from early intense activity, and development and maintenance of interpersonal relationships (Stebbins, 2001b). Some of its costs root in excessive casual leisure or lack of variety as manifested in boredom or lack of time for leisure activities that contribute to self through acquisition of skills, knowledge, and experience (i.e., serious leisure). Moreover, casual leisure alone is unlikely to produce a distinctive leisure identity.

Project-Based Leisure

Project-based leisure (Stebbins, 2005a)—a third form of leisure activity—requires considerable planning, effort, and sometimes skill or knowledge, but is ultimately neither serious leisure nor intended to develop into such. Examples include surprise birthday parties, elaborate preparations for a major holiday, and volunteering for sports events. Though only a rudimentary social world springs up around the project, it does, in its own particular way, bring together friends, neighbors, or relatives (e.g., through a genealogical project or Christmas celebration), or draw the individual participant into an organizational milieu (e.g., through volunteering for a sports event or major convention).

Types of Project-Based Leisure

It was noted in the definition just presented that project-based leisure is not all the same. Whereas systematic exploration may reveal others, two types are presently evident: one-shot projects and occasional projects. These are presented next using an earlier classificatory framework for amateur, hobbyist, and volunteer activities developed by the second author (see Stebbins, 1998, chaps. 2-4).

One-Shot Projects

In all of these projects, people generally use the talents and knowledge they have at hand, even though for some projects they may seek certain instructions beforehand, such as reading a book or taking a short course. Also, some projects resembling hobbyist activity participation may require a modicum of preliminary conditioning. The goal is to always successfully undertake the one-shot project and nothing more, and sometimes a small amount of background preparation is necessary for this. It is possible that a survey would show that most project-based leisure is hobbyist in character and the next most common, a kind of volunteering. First, the following hobbyist-like projects have been identified so far:
Making and tinkering:
- Interlacing, interlocking, and knot-making from kits.
- Other kit assembly projects (e.g., stereo tuner, craft store projects).
- Do-it-yourself projects done primarily for fulfillment, some of which may even be undertaken with minimal skill and knowledge (e.g., building a rock wall or a fence, finishing a room in the basement, planting a special garden). This could turn into an irregular series of such projects, spread over many years, possibly even transforming the participant into a hobbyist.

Liberal arts:
  • Genealogy (not as an ongoing hobby).
  • Tourism: a special trip, not as part of an extensive personal tour program, but rather to visit different parts of a region, a continent, or much of the world.
  • Activity participation: long back-packing trip, canoe trip; one-shot mountain ascent (e.g., Fuji, Rainier, Kilimanjaro)

One-shot volunteering projects are also common, though somewhat less so than hobbyist-like projects.
  • Volunteer at a convention or conference, whether local, national, or international in scope.
  • Volunteer at a sporting competition, whether local, national, or international in scope.
  • Volunteer at an arts festival or special exhibition in a museum.
  • Volunteer to help restore human life or wildlife after a natural or human-made disaster caused by, for instance, a hurricane, earthquake, oil spill, or industrial accident.

Less common than either are the amateur-like projects, which seem to concentrate in the sphere of theater.
  • Entertainment Theater: produce a skit (a form of sketch) or one-shot community pageant; create a puppet show; prepare a home film or a set of videos, slides, or photos; prepare a public talk.

Occasional Projects

The occasional projects seem more likely to originate in, or be motivated by, agreeable obligation (Stebbins, 2000a) than their one-shot cousins. Examples of occasional projects include the sum of the culinary, decorative, or other creative activities undertaken, for example, at home or at work for a religious occasion or someone's birthday. Likewise, national holidays and similar celebrations sometimes inspire individuals to mount occasional projects consisting of an ensemble of inventive elements.

Unlike one-shot projects, occasional projects have the potential to become routinized, which happens when new creative possibilities no longer come to mind as the participant arrives at a fulfilling formula wanting no further modification. North Americans who decorate their homes the same way each Christmas season exemplify this situation. Indeed, it can happen that, over the years, such projects may lose their appeal, but not their necessity, thereby becoming disagreeable obligations, which their participants no longer consider leisure.

To avoid being overlooked, it should be noted that one-shot projects also hold the possibility of becoming unpleasant. Thus, the hobbyist genealogist may become overwhelmed with the details of family history and the difficulty of verifying dates. The thought of putting in time and effort doing something once considered leisure, but which she now dislikes, makes no sense. Likewise, volunteering for a project may turn sour, creating a sense of being faced with a disagreeable obligation, which however, must still be honored. This is leisure no more.

Leisure Education

Charles Brightbill was one of the first scholars to acknowledge the importance of what he variously called "education for leisure" and "leisure education." He wrote that "when we speak . . . of education for leisure, we have in mind the process of helping *all* persons develop appreciations, interests, skills, and *opportunities* that will enable them to use their leisure in personally rewarding ways" (italics in original, Brightbill, 1961, p. 188). Given these words, it is safe to say that, were Brightbill writing today, he would argue that leisure education should center, for the most part, on serious leisure. In particular, such education should consist mainly of imparting knowledge about the nature of serious leisure, about its costs and rewards, and about participating in particular serious leisure activities. This conception of leisure education intentionally excludes casual leisure on the grounds that in order to engage in and find enjoyment in such leisure, little or no training or encouragement is required.

Yet, we have come to recognize that the idea of optimal leisure lifestyle certainly grants notable importance to casual leisure. The term refers to the deeply rewarding and interesting pursuit during free time of one or more substantial, absorbing forms of serious leisure, complemented by judicious amounts of casual leisure or project-based leisure if not both (Stebbins, 2000b; 2006a). People find optimal leisure lifestyles by partaking of leisure activities that individually and in combination help them realize their human potential, leading thereby to self-fulfillment and enhanced well-being and quality of life. This aim has to be connected with ethical education, which is to train people how to realize the part of humanity they are responsible for. All activities chosen have to be in relation with their potential of added value to humankind. Aristotle observes in *Nichomachean Ethics*, Book X, that the search for Happiness has much to do with reversing the order: It is not that quality of life will "provide" better people, but only that quality people can generate quality of life.

In line with this thinking, the goal of leisure education, as just presented, should be rephrased: that goal should be not only to inform clients or students about the nature of casual leisure but also to inform them about its role in a well-balanced, optimal leisure lifestyle. Leisure education includes helping people find the most appealing casual leisure available and effectively blend it with their serious and project-based leisure. Earlier we reviewed the components of casual leisure that leisure educators also need to consider: its benefits (Stebbins, 2001b; Hutchinson and Kleiber, 2005) and its capacity for promoting relaxation (Kleiber, 2000).

Since the general public is largely unaware of the concept of serious leisure, the first goal of educators for leisure—who when conceived of broadly include counselors, volunteers, and classroom instructors—is to inform their clients or students about its nature and value. Such information is important for anyone searching for an optimal leisure lifestyle: the pursuit of one or more substantial, absorbing leisure activities that taken alone or together approach the person's ideal of a fulfilling existence during free time. More particularly, such education should be composed of instruction on the nature of serious leisure, the general rewards (and costs) of such activity, the possibility of finding a leisure career there, and the variety of social and psychological advantages that can accrue to the person who pursues it (e.g., special identity, routine, lifestyle, organizational belonging, central life interest, membership in a social world). In some instances, people will have to be told how to get started in the pursuits of interest to them. Elsewhere, Stebbins (1998, chap. 6) provides information on how to do this in North America, which, however, may sometimes be inappropriate for other parts of the world. Thus, to more effectively guide the people they are working with, leisure educators outside North America may have to gather information on how to get started that is specific to their country and local community.

Plan of the Book

Chapter 2, written by Chris Rojek, provides the context within which we see leisure education operating, namely, in democratic society as situated in a milieu of social capital and civil labor. Risks and opportunities inhere in this milieu, which serves as a meeting place for citizens from diverse backgrounds. In the chapter 3, Cohen-Gewerc and Stebbins discuss the idea of leisure education itself: the ways it has changed over time, the role it plays in socializing the individual, and the nature of its present-day foundation. Atara Sivan extends these ideas in chapter 4, as she examines the differences between role training and development of individual capacity, as well as the process of learning to be free so as to be "busy" (in the positive sense of the word).

In chapter 5, Corinne Spector looks at leisure education through the lens of lifelong learning in childhood, adolescence, and young adulthood. In an era of great change and uncertainty, we must start learning at an early age to deal with increased freedom and greater responsibility than heretofore. Francis Lobo continues in chapter 6 with the theme of leisure education and lifelong learning, as both unfold in the early, middle, and later years of adults. Lifelong learning, as leisure, has the capacity to enhance quality of life along the entire span of life. Then, in chapter 7, Ian Patterson addresses the matter of leisure education for special groups and people with special needs. He includes in his analysis the "forced leisure" of unemployment and mandatory retirement, as well as the problem of boredom. In chapter 8, Karla Henderson discusses leisure education and its place in the various leisure industries. Here she confronts, among others, the questions of consumption and experience in the modern world. Cohen-Gewerc and Stebbins conclude by summing up the "common" principal themes considered in the earlier chapters. They then look at the new meaning of leisure, including its impact on family and community; the transition from free time to the Era of Leisure; and the matter of leisure, happiness, and well-being.

References

Brightbill, C. K. (1961). *Man and leisure: A philosophy of recreation*. Englewood Cliffs, NJ: Prentice-Hall.

The Economist (2005, October 20). Up off the couch. p. 35.

Hutchinson, S. L. and Kleiber, D. A. (2005). Gifts of the ordinary: Casual leisure's contributions to health and well-being. *World Leisure Journal, 47*(3), 2–16.

Kaplan, M. (1960). *Leisure in America: A social inquiry*. New York: Wiley.

Kleiber, D. A. (2000). The neglect of relaxation. *Journal of Leisure Research, 32*, 82–86.

Stebbins, R. A. (1982). Serious leisure: A conceptual statement. *Pacific Sociological Review, 25*, 251–272.

Stebbins, R. A. (1992). *Amateurs, professionals, and serious leisure*. Montreal, QC and Kingston, ON: McGill-Queen's University Press.

Stebbins, R. A. (1997). Casual leisure: A conceptual statement. *Leisure Studies, 16*, 17–25.

Stebbins, R. A. (1998). *After work: The search for an optimal leisure lifestyle*. Calgary, AB: Detselig.

Stebbins, R. A. (2000a). Obligation as an aspect of leisure experience. *Journal of Leisure Research, 32*, 152–155.

Stebbins, R. A. (2000b). Optimal leisure lifestyle: Combining serious and casual leisure for personal well-being. In M. C. Cabeza (Ed.), *Leisure and human development: Proposals for the 6th World Leisure Congress*. (pp. 101–107). Bilbao, Spain: University of Deusto.

Stebbins, R. A. (2001a). *Volunteering—mainstream and marginal: Preserving the leisure experience*. In M. Graham & M. Foley (Eds.), Volunteering in leisure: Marginal or inclusive? (Vol. 75, pp. 1–10). Eastbourne, UK: Leisure Studies Association.

Stebbins, R. A. (2001b). The costs and benefits of hedonism: Some consequences of taking casual leisure seriously. *Leisure Studies, 20*, 305–309.

Stebbins, R. A. (2001c). *New directions in the theory and research of serious leisure, Mellen Studies in Sociology, vol. 28*. Lewiston, NY: Edwin Mellen.

Stebbins, R. A. (2004a). Introduction. In R. Stebbins, and M. Graham (Eds.), *Volunteering as leisure/leisure as volunteering: An international assessment* (pp. 1–12). Wallingford, UK: CAB International.

Stebbins, R. A. (2004b). Pleasurable aerobic activity: A type of casual-leisure with salubrious implications. *World Leisure Journal, 46*(4), 55–58.

Stebbins, R. A. (2004c). Fun, enjoyable, satisfying, fulfilling: Describing positive leisure experience. *Leisure Studies Association Newsletter, 69*(November), 8–11.

Stebbins, R. A. (2005a). Project-based leisure: Theoretical neglect of a common use of free time. *Leisure Studies, 24,* 1–11.

Stebbins, R. A. (2005b). Choice and experiential definitions of leisure. *Leisure Sciences, 27,* 349–352.

Stebbins, R. A. (2006a). Discretionary time commitment: Effects on leisure choice and lifestyle. *Leisure Studies Association Newsletter, 74*(July), 18–20.

Stebbins, R. A. (2006b). *Serious leisure: A perspective for our time.* New Brunswick, NJ: AldineTransaction.

Unruh, D. R. (1980). The nature of social worlds. *Pacific Sociological Review, 23,* 271–296.

Chapter Two
Leisure and Neat Capitalism
by Chris Rojek

Neat capitalism is a type of market organization that recognizes ethical responsibilities at the levels of both the business corporation and the individual consumer. The fashionable business corporation accepts that making a profit involves giving something back to society. In concrete terms, this is expressed in ethical responsibilities in respect to the environment, health and distributive justice, and economic investment in community projects and education. At the level of the consumer, individuals accept responsibilities with regard to the personal monitoring of environmental, local, national, and global political and distributive issues. These responsibilities may involve no more than keeping regularly informed through the media, or they may extend to disciplined, organized consumer activism. Contemporary Western society is so saturated with the media that the only way that individuals can avoid being informed is by deliberately cutting themselves off from newsprint, broadcasting, and the internet.

Neat capitalism proceeds on the principle that the state no longer monopolizes national or global governance. Corporations and citizens decide for themselves on social, political, and environmental issues. As such, it appears to represent an extension of democracy. But this is more apparent than real, since corporations and activists do not answer to an electorate. Their accountability is to shareholders, consumers, and fellow activists, rather than to society at large. This constitutes a new form of intervention into public life and requires us to rethink social capital as something that is invested at the corporate level, as well as at the level of the individual.

The redefinition of corporate governance in the era of neat capitalism acknowledges that the corporation has a duty to engage with ethical issues relating to the environment and consumers. Embracing these issues may take a variety of forms. In some cases it may involve initiating and managing relief campaigns to disaster-struck or economically disadvantaged areas. The Body Shop, Virgin, Calvin Klein, Apple, Microsoft, and Starbucks Coffee have engaged in activities of this sort, and a study of their annual company reports will show the extent and variety of their activities. Ethical corporate governance may also take the form of education and health campaigns designed to inform consumers of the relationship between certain types of lifestyle, environmental stability, and personal well-being.

For the citizen, neat capitalism is founded upon the principle of the active consumer; that is, a consumer who regularly keeps informed about issues relating to consumption, the global environment, and international justice, or who has knowledge of the means to acquire this information. Leisure is crucial in finding out about the state of the world through watching television, reading the press, browsing the Internet, or talking with like-minded others. Through these means the active consumer acquires data that may conflict with the outlook of the state and the corporation. In the sense in which the author is using it, consumer activism is an unavoidable part of participating in consumer culture. This is because, even if one attempts to "switch off," the media offer a continuous flow of data on issues of social inclusion, social exclusion, distributive justice, health, and the environment.

The core idea of neat capitalism is corporate and personal engagement beyond the direct interests of the corporation or the individual to encompass the context in which corporate and individual activities occur. Making the world a better place and improving your life and the lives of those around you are basic imperatives of corporate strategy and lifestyle choice. These issues extend beyond the workplace and the leisure setting to constitute strategies that influence corporate governance, lifestyle strategy, and politics. However, it is as if the state is tacitly regarded to be cumbersome and unwieldy because it is assumed to be fatally wrapped up in red tape. The real action is in the unregulated partnership between corporations and consumers to address real world issues and provide fast, no-nonsense solutions to local, national, and global problems.

Live Aid, Virgin, and Wal-Mart

A high profile example that gained massive international coverage was the Live Aid event in July of 1985. This multi-venue music festival was organized by the British pop stars Bob Geldof and Midge Ure. It involved concerts at Wembley Stadium, London (attended by about 72,000 people) and JFK Stadium, Philadelphia (attended by about 92,000 people), with lesser events in Sydney and Moscow. The concerts were relayed throughout the world with one of the biggest ever live television link-ups, involving 100 countries, with an estimated 1.5 billion viewers. Live Aid was based on a philosophy that appealed to individual conscience about the consequences of famine in Ethiopia. It was combined with an aggressive commitment to cash aid from Western consumers to subsidize income flow to state relief, which was widely perceived as inadequate. In many ways it provided a model for neat capitalism, combining the energies of ordinary citizens with corporate financial pledges to make the world a better place. Bob Geldof emerged as the face of Live Aid, and his direct, personal commitment to the disaster in Ethiopia became the template for neat industrial capitalists (e.g., Steve Jobs [Apple], Bill Gates [Microsoft], Anita Roddick [The Body Shop], and Richard Branson [Virgin]) to emulate. Their style is informal, unstuffy, and focused on evidence-based methods to solve real world problems.

A good recent corporate example is the response of Richard Branson's Virgin Group to the 2004 tsunami disaster in South East Asia. The scale of this catastrophe generated widespread discussion among Western citizens about the necessity for aid and relief. The media was pivotal in informing citizens about conditions in the worst affected areas and the inadequate assistance offered from Western governments and non-governmental organizations. Public opinion suggested that traditional channels of disaster relief were too slow and inflexible. Virgin was one of a group of corporations that engaged to offer pragmatic, nongovernmental solutions to the problem. Virgin diverted part of its fleet of planes and instructed them to distribute food and medical supplies to the worst hit areas. Although it presented itself as working in conjunction with nongovernmental organizations, it implied that its "can do" approach was more responsive and relevant.

Another example is the new disaster-response partnership between Wal-Mart and the Red Cross, announced in 2006. This partnership was established in reaction to the U.S. government's lamentable response to Hurricane Katrina in 2005. The U.S. government is widely regarded to have been negligent in providing adequate disaster relief to New Orleans and the surrounding region. In particular, the Department of Homeland Security has been roundly criticized for being inefficiently managed with an over-reliance on casualized labor. The private sector is widely perceived to be more effective in its management structure.

These nongovernmental interventions may have a real life and death impact upon the locations on which they focus. But there are wider consequences that benefit the corporation. In the first place, the impression of relevance is an asset to these corporations in the global marketplace.

In contemporary capitalism, impression is everything. The reality of performing well in disaster-hit or under-privileged regions of the world has a demonstration effect, worth millions of dollars that would otherwise be spent in advertising campaigns for the corporations concerned. This is useful in consolidating and advancing their position in relation to market share.

Secondly, partnerships between private corporations and charities are often the thin end of the wedge to securing contract work paid for out of public funds. For example, the Shaw Group based in Baton Rouge, Louisiana, offering services in engineering, construction, environmental, and industrial operations, has been a major recipient of public grants to cope with the aftereffects of Katrina.

The recent conflicts in Afghanistan and Iraq have supplied a different set of dramatic business opportunities for American companies who express the rhetoric of adding value to the globe. For instance, according to the Center for Public Integrity, the Bechtel Group received $1.03 billion from the U.S. Agency for International Development to repair basic services in Iraq. The Environmental Chemical Corporation—specializing in decontamination, asbestos clean up, groundwater treatment, and cleaning up radioactive and explosive waste—received a one year contract for repair work in Iraq from the U.S. Department of Defense, with four option years that could eventually be worth $1.475 billion. KBR (formerly Kellogg, Brown and Root, a subsidiary of Halliburton) was awarded $7 billion for development work in Iraq in a deal achieved without submission for public or congressional approval. An Army spokesperson cited the classified status of the work as the pretext for avoiding open bidding.

In effect, all of these contracts are a form of outsourcing in which the public sector transfers responsibilities and funding to the private sector. However, the taxpayer foots the bill.

Neat Capitalism, Social Capital, and Leisure

Neat capitalism and the savvy consumer go hand in hand: The partnership has reformed many aspects of traditional capitalism. The arrangement is a variation of Robert Putnam's (2000) model of social capital. Putnam argued that a good deal of essential labor in society is unaccounted for and unpaid. This is because it consists of voluntary labor that is dispersed in the form of a gift relationship to others. I have a friend who is challenged by almost any form of household repair. If the flush mechanism on the toilet breaks or a sink gets blocked, he is unable to fix it himself. Fortunately, he has a next door neighbor who is a handyman. When my friend has a problem, the next-door neighbor generally fixes it. He never accepts the offer of payment. He regards his free voluntary labor as part and parcel of being a good neighbor.

This is a concrete example of what Putnam means by social capital. It adds to the common value, but has no economic cost. Other examples might include mowing the lawn of an elderly person, shopping for a handicapped person, minding a friend's children, or cleaning a public green space of weeds. If offered on a contractual basis, all of these activities would involve payment. That they are donated voluntarily in the spirit of community goodwill saves individuals money and relieves society of the burden of providing these services.

A good deal of free voluntary labor expended in the maintenance and development of social capital is concentrated in leisure time. The expenditure of voluntary labor to do good for others or benefit the environment can be a source of pleasure for both the donator and recipient of labor. For the donator, the line between leisure and voluntary labor may often be a thin one. This raises the question of considering how much leisure is allocated to the maintenance and governance of social capital in society. The methods of measuring this are imperfect, and common sense suggests that the allocation of leisure to this end is significant. Putnam certainly thinks so, and contends that expanding the share of leisure in society that is used in this way should be encouraged as a public benefit.

However, if outsourcing represents a significant saving for the state, how should one view the use of leisure in providing stateless solutions to social problems? By addressing social, economic, environmental, and disaster-relief concerns, neat capitalism may fill a gap that the state is deficient in filling. Conversely, the participation of charities and citizens in partnership with corporations that follow a social agenda plainly enhances the market position of the corporation by providing free advertising and the peripheral benefit of publicly funded contracts that ensue from a "can do" approach. As with the significance of voluntary labor that maintains and develops social capital, which is discharged in leisure, it is very difficult to estimate the contribution to the balance sheet of neat capitalist corporations that is derived from the voluntary expenditure of labor in the leisure time of citizen's. In all likelihood, the contribution is colossal.

Neat capitalism adds a new layer to the old Marxist model of exploitation. According to Marxists, corporations exploit consumers by offering them goods and services that are more expensive than they need to be and by forcing the majority to contract their labor power out in the form of paid labor. The capitalist justifies the difference between the cost of offering a good or service and the price charged to the consumer for consuming it by deeming it the reward for "enterprise." But enterprise is a very gray concept. There is no agreed upon way of formulating the value of enterprise. In general, it is established by what the market can bear.

The new layer of consumer exploitation involved in neat capitalism is the discharge of consumer voluntary labor, typically in the leisure sphere, which operates indirectly to consolidate the market position of the corporation through providing free advertising, and may directly lead to significant peripheral contracts. Activism and the consumer rights movement have exposed many of the defects and abuses of capitalism. Since activists and consumer rights movements form a prominent part of the market, corporations have been forced to listen to them and to amend their practices and business strategies. The result has not been the fundamental transformation of capitalism to produce a fairer, more democratic deal for consumers. Rather, it has been to reform capitalism by consolidating its position as a system that has "no alternative." By portraying the corporation as a more efficient global problem solver than the state, neat capitalism presents capitalism as the most responsive social system imaginable. However, it does not require capitalists to abandon the traditional function of generating profit for executives and shareholders. On the contrary, the rhetoric of neat capitalism presents profit as correlating with the superior relevance and efficiency of neat capitalist organization. Thus, the unintended consequence of environmental and political activism may be to outwardly reform corporations and to create new opportunities for growth which enhance competitive advantage and consolidate the grip of capitalism in individual, community, national, and global life.

Neat Capitalism in Practice: Automakers and Alcohol Manufacturers

Consider two concrete examples in the field of leisure: the response of automakers to the environmental lobby and the reaction of alcohol companies to the health risks cited in connection with drinking.

Automobiles and Global Warming

The relationship between driving for pleasure and environmental pollution is well-documented. The role of environmental activists and protest groups has been crucial in enhancing public awareness of the issue. The National Society for Clean Air and Environmental Protection (NSCA) in the UK submits that road transport accounts for 22 percent of total UK emissions of carbon dioxide, which is a major contribution to climate change. According to a report on pollution and global warming produced by the nonprofit organization, Environmental Defense in June of 2006, America plays a disproportionate role in contributing to the problem. Americans represent 5 percent of the world's population but drive 30 percent of the world's cars which, in turn, account for nearly 45 percent of the carbon dioxide pumped into the atmosphere each year. In contrast, emissions from light vehicles in Europe are estimated to account for 27 percent of greenhouse gas pollution. The problem caused by American vehicles is compounded because they are typically less fuel efficient, emitting on average, 15 percent more carbon dioxide. Americans drive 202 million passenger vehicles out of 683 million worldwide. The average U.S. passenger vehicle, with a fuel economy of less than 20 mpg, travels 11,000 miles per year. Moreover, Americans are commuting more each year. Between 1990 and 2001 the number of miles traveled increased by 40 percent.

A good deal of this travel is conducted in Sports Utility Vehicles (SUVs). The sale of SUVs is declining as a result of increasing fuel prices. Paradoxically, SUVs are likely to have a bigger share of road traffic in the future, as older, smaller cars are consigned to the scrapheap. At the time of this printing, more SUVs are sold in the U.S. than any other type of car. It is predicted that SUVs will be the main source of automotive CO_2 emissions, emitting the equivalent of 55 large coal-fired power plants. Automobiles account for a tenth of the world's greenhouse gas emissions, and American light vehicles are responsible for 20 percent of U.S. energy-related emissions.

A major target of environmentalists in this area has been GM (General Motors), on the grounds that it is lax in producing more fuel efficient, environmentally friendly engines. GM is the leading automaker in the U.S. Their output in 2004 was estimated to produce CO_2 emissions that are equivalent to the level produced by the American Electric Power Company, the largest operator of coal-fire plants. Like most other automakers, GM is committed to addressing environmental concerns. GM's website includes company reports and an environmental mission statement to "Protect human health, natural resources and the global environment." The environmental report meets the criticisms of environmentalists directly by conceding that GM products and manufacturing facilities produce CO_2 emissions and greenhouse gases. GM addresses this through the development of new technologies, partnerships with environmental organizations (such as the Nature Conservancy), and process improvements. The report goes on to claim that between 1990 and 2005, greenhouse gas emissions produced by GM vehicles dropped 77.2 percent, and that the emissions from its manufacturing facilities fell by 27.3 percent. However, the problem is not the rate of decline, since the 1990 rate was unregulated and had already contributed to hazardous global warming. The problem is the continuing role of GM as a flagrant, primary polluter of the environment. This role is tacitly accepted by GM, but it is obscured by trumpeting the corporation's version of corporate responsibility with respect to the global environment. To put it differently, GM presents itself as a neat capitalist company dedicated to preserving and improving the environment, health, and well-being of individuals. In response to the environmental lobby it has reduced its production of CO_2 emissions. But this is a smokescreen that disguises the corporation's role in adding to CO_2 emissions and global warming as an ordinary, inevitable part of its business.

Alcohol Manufacturers

The Anheuser-Busch Group of companies (AB) account for 57 percent of U.S. ale beverage consumption. In 2005, Anheuser-Busch shipped 1010 million barrels—more than 2.5 times than that of its closest domestic competitor. Anheuser-Busch has 48.8 percent of the U.S. market share, which includes the Budweiser, Bud Light, and Michelob brands. Its version of corporate governance is expressed in its company report, and is similar to the GM strategy in accepting the case of the environmental and health lobbies that its product base can be harmful. It emphasizes the duty of consumers to be responsible in their consumption patterns. "Budweiser Means Moderation" is the tagline for one of its most popular brands. Anheuser-Busch claims to have invested in alcohol awareness and education initiatives since the early 1900s. Through community-based programs, partnerships, and personal responsibility campaigns, Anheuser-Busch claims to have participated in the 37 percent reduction in drunk-driving fatalities listed by the U.S. Department of Transportation from 1982-2000. The Anheuser-Busch war on underage drinking is singled out as a particularly notable success. The 1999 "We All Make a Difference" campaign reinforced personal responsibility and warned consumers of the dangers involved in alcohol abuse, drunk driving, and underage drinking. Anheuser-Busch works directly with the National Social Norms Resource Center to underwrite education programs at U.S. colleges and universities, which stress that college students of legal age must drink responsibly if they choose to drink.

Anheuser-Busch has developed a variety of responsible environmental and community initiatives including recycling, solid waste reduction, "partners in progress" programs with minority and women-owned vendors, health mobile screening units, animal rescue campaigns, breast cancer cure research, disaster relief, and Paralyzed Veterans of America (PVA). It has developed a high profile entertainment and leisure park program through its Busch Gardens parks in Williamsburg, VA and Tampa, FL.

The world's fastest-growing and largest beer market by volume is China. Anheuser-Busch has made significant market investment to build recognition of its Budweiser brands there. It has a 27 percent equity position in Tsingato, the largest brewer in China and producer of the Tsingato brand. Anheuser-Busch also owns 50 percent of Mexico's leading brewer, Grupo Modelo, which has a 56 percent share of the Mexican beer market.

Although beer outsells hard liquor and wine in the U.S., its rate of growth has been depressed by the increasing popularity of these beverages with the U.S. consumer. Anheuser-Busch consolidated sales declined by 0.5 percent in 2005. The 2006 company plan is committed to enhance domestic beer volume and market share growth, including new product development, packaging, and promotions. Although the ethic of responsible drinking is reinforced, the aim of the 2006 plan is to increase volume sales. With respect to the domestic market this means that a) either more people need to consume the Anheuser-Busch brands or b) the current market needs to consume in greater volume. Revenues can also be increased globally by entering new markets. Anheuser-Busch may do this under the banner of "responsible drinking." However, there is no guarantee that consumers in the emerging and developing world, where a lower proportion of Gross National Product is devoted to health awareness and education campaigns, will observe the health warnings.

A variety of chronic physical conditions and diseases are associated with the excessive consumption of alcohol. They include acute pancreatitis, liver cancer, stroke, esophageal cancer, gastroesophageal hemorrhage, liver cirrhosis, and hypertension. Among the acute conditions are alcohol poisoning, child maltreatment, fall injuries, fire injuries, homicide, motor-vehicle traffic injuries, and suicide. According to statistics supplied by the U.S. Center for Disease Control and Prevention's website, excessive alcohol consumption is the third leading preventable cause of death in the U.S. Approximately 75,000 alcohol-related deaths occur in the U.S. every year, with, on average, thirty years of life lost per individual. The majority of deaths (72 percent) involved young males (under 35 years of age). About half of the total deaths resulted from acute conditions.

Anheuser-Busch's ethic of responsible drinking is designed to minimize the potential negative impacts of alcohol misuse on individuals, their families, and the wider community. However, its business, what it does to stay in operation and make a profit, is producing a commodity that is associated with addiction, illness, and premature death. Especially among young people, moderation and alcohol do not go hand in hand. Advertising campaigns deliberately target the youth market. Research by Snyder, Milici, Slater, Sun, and Strizhakova (2006) in the U.S., discovered a direct correlation between advertising and significant increases in youth drinking. Young people, between the ages of 15 and 26, who reported seeing more alcohol advertisements drank more on average, with each additional ad seen increasing the number of drinks consumed by 1 percent. Similarly, young people living in media markets with greater alcohol advertising expenditures drank more, with each additional dollar spent per capita increasing the number of drinks consumed by 3 percent. To express it differently, a 20-year-old male who sees few alcohol ads and lives in a media market with minimal advertising expenditures per capita is estimated to consume nine alcoholic drinks per month, compared to 16 drinks per month if he were to see many ads. All of the piety in the world will not disguise the fact that Anheuser-Busch plays a major role in encouraging young people to drink. Among young people, exposure to alcohol is associated with alterations in brain development, poor academic performance, risky sexual behavior, increased likelihood of addiction, and increased probability of fatal alcohol-related accidents.

The Origins of Neat Capitalism

Neat capitalism is concentrated in the Western liberal democracies, although its effects are now evident throughout the global economy. Its origins can be traced back to the consumer counterculture of the 1960s. Although it was not exclusively concentrated in leisure, nonwork time and space played a significant role in exchanging, exploiting, and developing activist consciousness and organization. The movement is widely credited with increasing democracy in the West. This was certainly its intended consequence. However, one of the unintended consequences was to supply corporations with ways of reforming themselves in order to strengthen market share and enhance capitalism.

Thomas Frank's (1997) book on the development of hip consumerism employs the example of the American advertising industry to illustrate how the counterculture/consumer rights movement transformed the face of capitalism. The traditional American advertising industry in the postwar period developed an array of quasi-scientific tools, based in survey research, motivational attitude scales, and opinion polls, designed to produce an objective model of lifestyle choice. The marketing emphasis was on commodities and services that would contribute to social progress. In the consumer culture of the day, the keystone of progress was technology. Commodities and services were invented, designed, and marketed to replace domestic labor, ease access from point A to B, and enhance lifestyle flexibility. In keeping with the logic of mass society, the advertising message had to be as simple as possible and repeated continuously in order to appeal to the largest number of people.

The Ted Bates Advertising Agency, which significantly increased market share in this period, emphasized the value of repetition, continuity, and adherence to a simple, accessible message based in the idea of a "unique selling proposition" (USP). USPs are intended to distinguish the product from the competition. One problem here is that many commodities in consumer culture are rather similar. What distinguishes brands of soap, toothpaste, or toilet paper from each other? For the Ted Bates Agency, it was what we would now call connotation. The advertising challenge is to create a set of associations with a product that make it different in the public mind from products of a similar type. One famous example was the USP for Colgate toothpaste. The Ted Bates campaign for Colgate claimed that Colgate "cleans your breath while it cleans your teeth." Clearly, this claim could be made on behalf of all toothpastes. However, by linking this claim specifically with Colgate, the Bates agency achieved a dominant share of the market in toothpaste products.

The example illustrates a number of features of traditional postwar capitalism. In the first place, it is based in a hierarchical model of consumer satisfaction. The corporation knows best. That is why it invests in quantitative and qualitative research to produce hard, scientific knowledge. Similarly, the wants of the consumer are assumed to be standardized, stable, and impressionable. Why else would a baseless tagline that only one toothpaste "cleans your teeth while it cleans your breath" be made? The governing assumptions correspond with the mass society model in social science of the day. This model proposed that individual taste and culture are fairly uniform. They are conditioned by the industrial-entertainment media to conform to the requirements of mass consumption.

The counterculture/consumer rights movement challenged this model of capitalism in many ways. It challenged the traditional postwar advertising model on the grounds that it produced a stifling model of American society. It argued that advertising narratives failed to represent ethnic diversity, minimized subcultural nonconformity and difference, and sought to validate the white, suburban, home-owning nuclear family as the norm in the U.S. It attacked the authority of what William H. Whyte (1956) called "the organization men" that ran, not only the advertising industry, but the whole of American society. The alternative was recognizing difference and diversity especially with respect to ethnicity, gender, and sexuality. With respect to consumer culture this boiled down to one simple edict: listen to the consumer. The counterculture/consumer rights axis forced traditional corporations to address wider issues than product satisfaction, because consumers were passionately interested in wider issues of social justice, social inclusion and exclusion, and environmental concerns. By incorporating these issues into revised philosophies of corporate governance, corporations demonstrated their relevance to the modern consumer.

To be clear, this was a genuinely democratizing moment in postwar history. The rise of neat capitalism resulted in a more flexible and open relationship between corporations and consumers. However, the unintended consequence of more flexibility and relevance was the empowerment of corporations to offer nongovernmental solutions to questions of work, leisure, lifestyle, and democracy, and thereby challenge the preeminence of the state in each of these fields.

Leisure, Education, and Advocacy

Does it matter that neat capitalism offers stateless solutions to questions of work, leisure, lifestyle, and democracy? Since the neoliberal revival of the Reagan-Thatcher 1980s, public faith in the state has diminished. The ease with which deregulation, privatization, and outsourcing have been accomplished seems to point to high levels of public tolerance for the philosophy of corporate solutions to public problems. In many eyes, the slow and inadequate response of the state and federal levels of government to the Hurricane Katrina disaster in 2005 provides a cogent symbol of the inability of the modern state to offer effective solutions to public ills. It might be objected that years of underinvestment in disaster-relief agencies made it inevitable that the state's response to Katrina would be inadequate. The counter to this objection is that successive election campaigns since the neoliberal revival have established the doctrine that the public will not tolerate high taxation. So long as this is the case, there will be pressures upon the state to outsource disaster relief, waste disposal, recreational facilities, and other functions.

Although corporations are only accountable to their shareholders, this does not necessarily mean that the nongovernmental solutions they offer to the world's problems are without benefit. Corporations are probably more flexible than state departments in dealing with some forms of international crises. Their role is likely to be secondary, but because they are often multinational organizations with employees on the ground in disaster hit areas, their channels of communication and powers of mobilization are often of a high order. However, there is a danger that corporations will revert to the role of feudal barons in determining what is right for their own people and the world without genuine public accountability.

The rules of the game have changed and leisure educators face some difficult questions. Putnam (2000) argued that local activism through leisure can be very effective in contributing to social capital. However, perhaps the biggest problems we face are global, not local. The various forms of risk identified by Ulrich Beck (1992), such as climate change, environmental pollution, nuclear catastrophe, terrorist action, and disease require global solutions.

Leisure educators have acknowledged global responsibilities. The main sources here are the Sao Paulo Declaration *Leisure in a Globalized Society* (1998) adopted by delegates who attended the 5th World Congress of the World Leisure and Recreation Association' in Sao Paulo, Brazil; and the *Charter For Leisure*, prepared in 1970, but substantially revised in 1979 and 2000. Included in the Sao Paulo Declaration are the following undertakings:

1. World Leisure must function as a worldwide, nongovernmental organization dedicated to discovering and fostering the conditions that permit leisure to serve as a force to optimize collective and individual lifestyle and well-being for all.
2. All persons have the right to leisure through economic, political, and social policies that are equitable and sustainable.
3. All persons have a need to celebrate and share our diversity in leisure.
4. All private and public sectors consider the threats of abuse to diversity and quality of leisure experiences caused by the local, national, and international consequences of globalization.
5. All private and public sectors consider the threats to the abuse and misuse of leisure by individuals (i.e., deviant and criminal behavior), which result from local, national, and international forces.
6. All private and public sectors ensure that policies are implemented to provide leisure education curricula and programs for school and community systems, as well as programs to train related voluntary and professional human resources.

7. Efforts be made to better understand the consequences of globalization for leisure through a coherent program of ongoing research.
8. Efforts be made to disseminate information on the costs and benefits to leisure from the several and profound forces of globalization.

The Charter for Leisure puts the following articles forward:

1. All people have a basic human right to leisure activities that are in harmony with the norms and social values of their compatriots. All governments are obliged to recognize and protect this right of its citizens.
2. The individual is his/her best leisure and recreational resource. Thus, governments should ensure the means for acquiring those skills and understandings necessary to optimize leisure experiences.
3. Individuals can use leisure opportunities for developing self-fulfillment, communities, and cultural identity, as well as for promoting international understanding, cooperation, and enhancing quality of life.
4. Governments should ensure the future availability of fulfilling leisure experiences by maintaining the quality of their country's physical, social, and cultural environment.
5. Citizens must have access to all forms of information about the nature of leisure and its opportunities, using it to enhance their knowledge and inform decisions on local and national policy.
6. Educational institutions must make every effort to teach the nature and importance of leisure and how to integrate this knowledge into personal lifestyle.

Few would take issue with these principles. The question is, how can they be implemented? If the principles are to be more than worthy rhetoric, they require concrete plans and the support of real world organizations. At this level, the design of leisure educators falls down. The various nongovernmental organizations associated with leisure have a crucial role in alerting the public to questions of inequality, injustice, and risk in leisure practice. Article 2 of the Charter for Leisure states, "Provisions for Leisure for the quality of life are as important as those for health and education. Governments should ensure their citizens a variety of accessible leisure and recreational opportunities of the highest quality."

However, scarcely any government in the West provides resources for leisure that are equivalent to the public provision of resources for health and education. If it is true that leisure is as important as health and education, there is a tremendous learning curve to overcome before it is fiscally, ethically, and practically recognized as such.

As leisure educators, we have clear knowledge of hazardous leisure practice. We know that tobacco, alcohol, and recreational drugs carry demonstrable health risks for the individuals who consume them. Equally, gas emissions from automobiles degrade the environment and raise ethical issues about driving for pleasure. In fact, a good deal of leisure practice is potentially harmful, not only to individual health, but environmental stability. We also know that exercise and a balanced diet correlate positively with good health. The UK Food Standards Agency recommends eight tips for a balanced diet: base your meals on starchy foods; eat lots of fresh fruit and vegetables; eat more fish; cut down on saturated meat and sugar; try to eat less salt—no more than 6g a day; get active and try to be a healthy weight; drink plenty of water; don't skip breakfast. This sort of information is much more abundant today than it was even 25 years ago.

Donatory Citizenship, Active Citizenship, and Nongovernmental Solutions

There has been a transformation in consumer culture from donatory citizenship to active citizenship. By the term donatory citizenship, the author refers to the traditional models of citizenship based on the principle that the state and business corporations combine to create a context in which individuals could choose lifestyle without being concerned about the implications of their choice. Although the individual made choices, the context in which choice selection occurred was regarded as conditioned by the state and the corporation. By contrast, active citizenship is based on the principle that individuals, charities, and other types of nongovernmental organizations can offer stateless solutions to private ills and public problems. Corporate responsibility under neat capitalism has emerged as a contribution from the industrial and business sector to these ends. They are forms of stateless strategy to questions of lifestyle, risk, and responsibility. The expansion of the media has coincided with the enlargement of public consciousness about these issues.

The media also presents contradictory messages. For example, the doctrine of responsible drinking has been enhanced by media support. At the same time, in films, television, and other forms of media entertainment and dissemination of information, alcohol consumption is linked with style, popularity, and cool. The public is caught in a bind on this issue. The doctrine of responsible drinking is endorsed. At the same time, the media represents excess drinking as a tolerable way of letting your hair down, blowing off steam, producing disinhibition which may lead to sexual activity, and even as a form of self-medication to deal with depression and stress. The question is where to draw the line. Neither corporations nor the state provide clear guidance on this issue. In practice, the matter is left as a subject for individual conscience.

The emergence of nongovernmental solutions to private ills and public problems requires leisure educators to change their game. Lobbying the state for leisure resources and increased leisure awareness has a long and respectable history. However, in the era of active citizenship, extensive lobbying occurs outside of the sphere of leisure education and charities, and is located instead in corporate intervention and local and international activism. What is required is for leisure educators to engage more fully with the opportunities provided to make leisure count with the public in ways that benefit the social good. One consequence of this is that leisure educators must become more political and more visible in local and global leisure.

To what extent should leisure professionals be advocates of the perils of leisure practice? The strong association with leisure as a positive life value means that there is a good deal of resistance to articulating the negative effects of leisure practice. Leisure educators are often defensive about this issue. Instead of confronting the connections between leisure forms and illness or physical decay, they tend to treat negative leisure forms as a pathology which requires intervention from medical or legal professionals, rather than leisure educators. For example, drinking and tobacco cultures cannot be addressed only at the level of the consumer. Leisure educators must engage directly with the providers of these leisure commodities and expose the double standards that, for example, allow the Anheuser-Busch brewing company to preach the doctrine of responsible drinking to college students, while devising ever-new ways of increasing alcohol sales.

We cannot disinvent alcohol, tobacco, or the internal combustion engine. Nor would we wish to, since the moderate use of these commodities is tolerable. The challenge lies at a different level: that is, in exposing and elucidating how neat capitalism positions consumers in the marketplace. More precisely, it lies in revealing the mechanisms that neat capitalism uses to combine ethical consumption with commodity production that risks personal health and environmental stability. This involves adding another layer to the "can-do" attitude shared by activists and neat capitalist corporations. In particular, it involves clarifying how voluntary labor in leisure connects with neat capitalist interventions to private ills and public problems. Further, it requires leisure educators to explore how the use of leisure enhances the position of capitalist corporations by identifying a positive image with the corporation in the public mind.

References

Anheuser-Busch. (2007). *2006 Annual Report*. Retrieved November 1, 2007, from http://www.anheuser-busch.com/investor_relations/report_annual.html

Beck, U. (1992). Risk society: Toward a new modernity. London and Thousand Oaks, CA: Sage Publications.

Environmental Defense. (2006, June 28). *Cars built by each of the big three emit more greenhouse gas than America's largest electric utility company, AEP*. Retrieved November 1, 2007, from http://www.environmentaldefense.org/pressrelease.cfm?ContentID=5310

Frank, T. (1997). *The conquest of cool*. Chicago: University of Chicago Press.

Food Standards Agency. (n.d.). *8 tips for eating well*. Retrieved November 1, 2007, from http://www.eatwell.gov.uk/healthydiet/eighttipssection/8tips/

General Motors. (2007). *2005/06 corporate responsibility report*. Retrieved November 1, 2007, from http://www.gm.com/corporate/responsibility/reports/06/600_environment/600.html

Putnam, R. (2000). *Bowling alone*. New York: Touchstone.

Snyder, L., Milici, F. F., Slater, M., Sun, H., and Strizhakova, Y. (2006). Effects of alcohol advertising exposure on drinking among youth. *Archives of Pediatrics and Adolescent Medicine 160*(1), 18–24.

The National Society for Clean Air and Environmental Protection. (n.d.). *Transport*. Retrieved November 1, 2007, from http://www.nsca.org.uk/pages/topics_and_issues/transport.cfm

The Center for Public Integrity. (n.d.). *Windfalls of war: Bechtel Group Inc*. Retrieved November 1, 2007, from http://www.publicintegrity.org/wow/bio.aspx?act=pro&ddlC=6

Whyte, W. (1956). *The organization man*. New York: Simon & Schuster.

Wikipedia (2007). Retrieved November 1, 2007, from http://en.wikipedia.org/wiki/Live_Aid

World Leisure. (1970). *Charter for leisure*. Retrieved November 1, 2007, from www.worldleisure.org/pdfs/charter.pdf

Chapter Three
The Nature of Leisure Education
by Elie Cohen-Gewerc and Robert A. Stebbins

Immanuel Kant, in his "Treatise about Pedagogy," made this basic observation: "Man can be a human being only through education." The question is what sort of education, for what kind of man, under what kind of life challenges? Education in this new Era of Leisure must be responsible for providing a solid initiation and training of the new generations on how to cope with the ever expanding "spaces of freedom" (Dumazedier, 1988, p. 240).

In chapter 1 we explored the nature of leisure and its principal types, and then in chapter 2, we examined the role of leisure and leisure education in the broader context of the development of social capital. Thus the stage is now set to consider, in detail, what we mean by leisure education. First, we describe how many educational systems are still modeled on the ancient era, and then we look at what education should be on the threshold of our new Era of Leisure.

The ideas presented here are consistent with Brightbill's definition of leisure education, which was presented in chapter 1 and repeated here for convenience: "the process of helping *all* persons develop appreciations, interests, skills, and *opportunities* that will enable them to use their leisure in personally rewarding ways" (italics in original, Brightbill, 1961, p. 188). Brightbill wrote about "education for leisure," when leisure was only a small, but growing part of life. Our interest—and his definition harmonizes well with it—is broader, however; we will discuss, as a fruitful adaptation to the new era, education for life, in which leisure plays a central role.

Introduction

When every culture is legitimate, when different behaviors are no longer seen as strange, and when even deviance uses the popular umbrella of relativism, it becomes difficult to maintain respect for moral norms. Discipline is also deeply affected, while social cohesion seems under serious threat. Social prostration will leave our collective destiny in the hands of chance and anonymous forces that aim to dominate the masses through all manner of temptation. As we can observe, two processes coexist in our Western world:

- A continuous and faster process of decadence, still devoted to some inheritance of Modernism that tends to an instrumental regulation of life, clear from any vision, confined to "now," and to functional and hedonistic needs.
- A convulsive return to the moral world of yesterday, with clear-cut definitions and high fences to prevent any influence from the agitated life around us. It is a sort of fundamentalism that aspires to a closed world, "our world," a controlled world within the world.

From an individual point of view, both ways are sterile. An existence limited to itself, or a life that is only a corridor towards the "other life"—both seem to be a life without hope. We refer, instead, to conscious hope (Gonzalez-Pecothe, 1951/1978) that accompanies the efforts of those who are looking for meaning in their proper life and for the meaning of life as a whole. Both the eternal frozen signification of fundamentalism and the impossible sense of relative hedonism make real life burdensome and quite superfluous.

What is the difference between one who walks far away, on the fringe of life that runs on with all its rich complexity, and one who is submerged in life, experiencing excitement, but being unable to create the essential distance from where it is possible to distinguish and understand, and then add the essence of one's intimate experiences to one's cognition?

Conventional Education of the Old Era

Human history is the history of all the attempts to reduce, induce, and adapt the vibrations of life to the dimensions of common people, and to fix it. In this regard "happiness" was seen as "essentially narcosis, numbness, rest, quiet (Sabbath), mental relaxation and bodily relaxation, in a word, passivity" (Nietzsche, 1887/1985). The purpose was to close off life and fix its tracks to make it foreseeable, thereby freeing people of the burden of their personal freedom. Defined and enclosed life sets limits, but also brings identity, stability, and security. This results in a predictable and secure future. The verb "to contain" means to limit but also "to include" or "to comprise."

This model suits stable periods, when changes are quite imperceptible or, during the implementation of a new society issuing from a successful revolution, when a new world must emerge on the ruins of an ancient one. Concepts in stable periods are clear-cut; worthy of man whose human models are available in town squares and class textbooks. This is a simplified world painted only in black and white and hides a generally vague and collective sensation of debility. We can feel this in the hard intolerance toward non-normative behavior and different groups. Paradoxically, with real security comes curiosity and interest about accessible alternatives that gain greater legitimacy. Little by little we can see more people escaping the traditional dichotomy of a black-and-white world; they find they must choose either to live as everybody around them or to disappear from the larger community.

This phenomenon of escaping the traditional dichotomy will only be reinforced by the very new element carried on by the new era: that of individual free time. With increasing free time, individual autonomy grows and minds open with regards to personal choices in a new, richer reality.

Two critical questions then arise:

1. What remains from this false security engendered by a clear-cut worldview, when all of society is invaded by the numerous, pervasive influences of the global market? We know, for example, that with the economic and consumer items come wide-ranging cultural and social implications.
2. How can educational systems, today still prisoners of the ancient monotheistic model, educate and train young pupils who must be able to make their own decisions in a complex society that is widely influenced by the world market economy? The aims of this economy are clearly economic, whereas their consequences are mostly social and cultural.

We must remember that our common Western culture rests on monotheism—one God, one faith—in which choice is merely theoretical. Though we are largely unaware of them, these religious roots are still very much present in our schools. Thus, we can understand the schools' impotence, when confronted with "all these pagan consumer offers," which reach everyone directly wherever they are, as conveyed by the mass media.

Although there have been several reforms and new trends, education still has no life expectancy. It continues its uninterrupted erosion through double meanings, with hidden or stammered messages on the one hand, and passive acceptance of what happens here and now on the other. It is both interesting and sad to observe how conformist patterns—a deeply ingrained characteristic of education—prevent it from real change, while nevertheless pushing its members toward the slope of permissiveness. All the efforts to add sophisticated devices, and all the refinement of this anachronistic institution will not help if teachers still stand up, helpless and ignorant of what justifies their presence in the classroom and the invasion during 50 minutes of the lives of the pupils sitting there.

Neither finding these patterns in another world, nor preparing these teachers for a different "battle" (Aragon, 1946) can constitute the mental and effective environment in which young people can learn and train themselves to realize their compulsory and personal freedom (Sartre, 1943). In other words, how do people learn to choose one of the alternatives and take responsibility for their choice? In this new Era of Leisure, we no longer have the opportunity to deny personal liberty (Fromm, 1941). Children nowadays must make more decisions in a month than all the decisions their forefathers made a hundred years ago in their entire lives.

A large space, which is becoming increasingly wider, has now been opened to the sole control of the individual, beyond any institution and beyond any member of any hierarchy (Beck & Gernsheim-Beck, 1966). In this personal free space, one must make choices, when every decision means renouncement to other alternatives and above all, an intimate responsibility. Every individual is now abandoned to his or her own freedom. We are far from the collective umbrella of the illusion called "common responsibility"; it is hard now to escape into the shelter of "we," as in "we all decide," or "we (the ethnic group) do it this way," or "our tradition dictates." Nowadays, people feel, in every decision, the whole burden of their responsibility. Eighty years ago, Martin Buber wrote: "Within the fluctuations of the concept 'freedom,' arose the personal accountability which has nothing to lean on; not on any church, not on any society, or on any civilization. This is Responsibility standing alone in the Creation." (1925/1980, p. 260). Bergson stressed earlier (1913/1927) that Freedom cannot be free from rationality, nor can it be an unconscious devotion to instincts freed from social norms. Can we see graduates from our educational systems operating within this kind of freedom? Schools as they are cannot and will not be able to confront the challenge of our new Era. We need a different model, rather than more of the same "new" variations of the old.

As we saw, the challenge is to deal with the increasing importance of free time in individual life, where one is freed from all known and secure tracks—the essential issue of personal freedom. We must conceive of the existential experience that everybody has in every moment, everywhere, while surrounded by innumerable alternatives, some of which are truly fulfilling activities, while many others are merely hedonic temptations.

In our Western world, it is hard to ask most people to devote themselves to a collective identity and ever harder to ask that they sacrifice for it. People perceive themselves as different from everyone else. There are no longer any clear-cut definitions, and all the ways and trends, even those which do not yet exist, seem to be open. What kind of a liberty is this? It is hard to understand how, in such a reality, free from compulsory choices, from submission to homeland, to job, or even to gender, people feel and say: "There is nothing to do," while being ensnared in a dead end, feeling impotent and hopeless, with personal freedom negated.

It is quite simple: Most of the time, people have failed to free themselves from the norms and beliefs that have guided their lives. Rather, they have lost those norms and beliefs. People, immersed in their own emptiness, available to all offers and to all temptations, are nonetheless occasionally aware of how they are passive targets of all kinds of manipulation.

This confusion does not stop at the threshold of the schools. The typical teacher coming alone into a classroom, powerless, escapes into a sort of instrumental pedagogy, trying to survive the growing insolence of the assembled pupils. The teacher often fails to see that these children, beyond their agitation and lack of discipline, are like all human beings: they are experimenting with a deep and unconscious expectation for something that could inspire them toward achieving a level of consistent meaning in their own existence.

We can go on and sharpen school criticisms, strip political designs, and expose hidden social manipulations. It is also possible to join reform groups, whose essential purpose is to make learning more effective, as shown by success on standardized exams—learning which, however, continues to give us graduates who are ignorant.

But, are we able to foresee a new way of thinking, once out from under the dark shadow of superficial psychologism? We need a new vision with a different approach, by which a person will be able to learn how to construct his or her part of humanity in a society where all landmarks have been distorted. This is the real challenge for education in the new Era of Leisure. Put simply, we need a new kind of socialization.

Socialization

In a world that seemed immutable, socialization within a tightened network of common values could be simply the transmission of knowledge and a detailed repertoire of canonic behaviors. Later, with growing changes and improved technologies, schools had to adapt, and alongside traditional information, were forced to teach pupils how to get information and how to update it. In the new Era, however, we need something else; we must know how to change, that is, how to "become."

For a long time, Modernism's believers thought that all the amazing changes of the day influenced only the facilities for a better life, but not the basic concepts of life. Full of euphoria for "progress," they were enraptured by the illusion that external refinement meant internal improvement.

But how can we believe that only the convenience of life changes when people can move more often and to more remote destinations, when radios can transmit every event in real time, when products and ideas travel faster and faster? How can we consider free time as a negligible appendix of work? Can we not see the increase in time remaining after work and the many and varied family and social obligations that occupy this time? How aware are we of this crucial situation—that one can and must choose, whether within or outside the canonical patterns? Like the proverb "even the most beautiful woman can only give what she has to give," we understand that in every moment one can only confront a specific situation with what he or she has.

We can administer one's free time—this growing part of existence—only with the means we have in any given moment. "And there is a great difference between vacuity stemming from a poor being and vacuity resulting from over-vitality" (Laloup, 1969, p. 69). Under-vitality subordinates personal freedom to circumstances, and as a result, leisure degenerates into convulsive diversion or brutalization. On the contrary, with high-vitality one can experiment with a fruitful abundance, where leisure becomes a continuous encounter with oneself as one who wants and can take responsibility for one's "becoming."

It follows that the main responsibility for education now is to initiate and train our youth such that they will first develop, and then profit, from their own high-vitality. We have already said that there is no difference between the loneliness of people trapped in a defined and identifiable collective identity, and those in isolation in which they are swept away in anonymous crowds. So this new education has to be what vital and honest education must be: education for freedom, which means education leading one, not only to do and to consume, but to "be."

Leisure Education

How can leisure tools give us basic elements for this new training? What is leisure education?

The aim of leisure education must be to teach and train people how to choose, that is, how to change. Such education must offer youth opportunities to sense, distinguish, catch, and understand. It may also lead them to understand the concept of liberty, which emerges in meaningful encounters between the inner self and the world. It must invite them to undertake, by themselves, their own metamorphosis. Rather than being a manipulated object, youth may become a subject capable of taking initiatives, responding, and deciding; that is, to sense and to understand, to be separate and together, to decide while all paths are still open, to live without burning out one's vitality, to be and become, much as this occurs in artistic expression.

"Artistic creation is an attempt towards uniqueness. It appears as a complete thing, an absolute presence, and at the same time it belongs to a complex network of links. It issues from independent deed, it realizes a superior and free dream, but it funnels in all the energies of civilizations. It is material and it is spirit, it is shape and it is content" (Focillon, 1943, p.1). Just like an artist views all the colors available for his or her creation, individuals can see the many opportunities offered within free time like an infinite palette from where they can choose the tonalities that fit their own selves. Thus, they can aspire toward their personal fulfillment.

Leisure education enables people to meet all the potentialities of life, as life runs in every direction, with all its connections and unknown futures. Simply put, leisure education goes beyond educating and shaping people for roles in factories, organizations, communities, and politics. It can also empower the individual as a whole and autonomous being.

How to Become

The empowering process in this new education will offer every pupil the opportunity to become familiar with a fascinating world filled with numerous stimuli and processes. By becoming familiar in this way, the pupil will be able to experience a personal "becoming": something impossible if left to the passive forces of change through chance circumstances. Simply put, thanks to this new education, pupils will be able to enter the "workshop" of life without getting lost. Similarly, artists do not know in advance which colors will ultimately be found on the white canvas before them, but they do know that they will participate in a fruitful dialogue with the innumerable colors in the palette of existence.

The following is a brief example of the experience of a writer.

She sits before a blank sheet. She is both excited and anxious. She is excited because, on this page, some part of the trembling agitation of her whole being is expecting to come to light; feelings and pictures, still foggy, lie at this unique confluence of her existence, the point at which this intersection is occurring, that will always be a once-in-a-lifetime confrontation between what she has accumulated in her consciousness until this moment in time, and the present moment of existence, in which she looks both around and within herself.

The body is subject to chaos: to sights and feelings, sounds and smells, thoughts and colors, memories and longings, and the connections between all of these. The body exerts its senses and mobilizes its wisdom, and though the moment is passing, its passion seeks the absolute and the eternal. It is from here that both the excitement and anxiety stem. Every feeling, every sight that is revealed to the spirit's eyes bursts forth in its desire to be. However, in order to be, there is a need to take form. Forms come and go, arise and fade, between the feelings, the thoughts, the picture that exists in one's mind and the white page. The anxiety is great: so much excited vitality revolves around the tip of the pencil in the artist's hand, and yet the page remains blank.

Suddenly, a sentence is written, and is immediately present. Like the initial paint-stroke on an empty canvas, the sentence asks not just for consideration but demands partnership. The person is no longer alone with herself; the dialogue has begun. Slowly the page fills; the mental images, and foggy feelings take shape, the words condense into combinations, and the text creates an image of its own. It is as though the lines write themselves under some kind of enchanted spell by the author. The creation is here, though it has been born via the coupling between what has been noticed in one's internal world and what can be seen by the world around. Still, it is now an entity unto itself.

The artist looks, contemplates things around herself and inside herself, and finds that everything has changed. It appears, in 'objective' terms, according to outside observers, as though nothing has happened, though among the mirrors spread before herself and within herself, there is now a new entity. The artist's perspective has now broadened.

The first step in leisure education is rehabilitation of the look. To see, or observe, is found at the beginning, and also at the end, heralding a new start in a creative cycle. First we see, then we look, which gives us something to contemplate, and through contemplation we find new things to see.

Let us compare this process with the experience of the copyist in the Middle-Ages. Imagine a dutiful person very concerned to make no errors as he copies thousands of words. His only job is to copy the piece of art already there. Nothing that happens during this segment of life can have any effect upon the final work. The copyist's only mission is to duplicate, not to create. By contrast, an artist's concern is quite different. The artist aspires to express something unique: his or her self.

These examples can illustrate the difference between the past and the New Era. In the ancient era, people had to reproduce, in their own lives, the canonic and established patterns. Nowadays, we do not have to do this. Instead, we must choose from the multiplicity of stimuli and processes, from the chaos in and around ourselves, to create a new order, a unique composition: the single text of our personal existence.

Like artists, we are in charge of our ultimate mission: to create our own lives. Like an artistic endeavor, we must look at, not just see, what we are observing. Here, unlike in the past, memory and recognition are insufficient. Rather we need all our human faculties: observation, imagination, intuition, discernment, and prophecy. Free time opens our vision, and invites us to discover the abundant aspects of every moment, with its multiple associations and potential links.

To be prepared for life, one must enter "the future with full hands" (Gonzalez-Pecotche, 1951/1978, p. 273). This does not mean, however, being conditioned by ready-made scenarios. No prewritten script can entirely fit our tumultuous reality. To be able to step with self-confidence means to move through life with an empowered capacity of observation: "There is only one emotion: the sensation of strangeness; there is only one lyricism: the one which arises from renovating existence" (Paul Cezanne in Cachin F. & Rishel J., 1995, p. 34).

Once inspired by the openness of free time, we must understand that our days, weeks, and years are not standard, duplicated items. Each new moment is a concrete challenge for innovation. Innovation flourishes at the meeting point between all the elements we discover around us and the echo within our inner self to which the innovation corresponds. This self—our intimate interiority—is no longer under threat by canonic patterns or sterile skepticism. Furthermore, innovation is not necessarily showy change; rather, it can be some nuance added to personal aware-ness, one humble little step toward one's growing consciousness.

In other words, we can say that life in this new Era is a perpetual search. Instrumental routine is, of course, the basis of survival, but from here, we can, and must, sail toward all the aspects of life both around and within us. While sailing beyond the instrumental routine, we must be present, totally present; that is, we must be intimately connected with all the aspects of life we are experiencing. Indeed, after rehabilitating the "look," a critical issue for leisure education is how to train pupils to improve their capacity to be entirely present. During this voyage we are far, far away from leisure as distraction, from casual leisure, in which un-aware people waste their time and hence their lives. Clearly, in this new Era, praxis and theory (reflection) are intertwined (Gonzalez-Pecotche, 1957/1984).

Leisure of the serious variety, as set out in chapter 1, has to do with a quality vision of existence. Leisure education has much to do with qual-ity and uniqueness, and less to do with quantity and frenetic consumption that feeds a poor and alienated narcissism. Its goal is to train youth to im-prove their individual capacity to realize their part in humankind, which includes their part in the world and their personal commitment to human solidarity. This is a new concept of solidarity, which goes far beyond political, ethnic, and other kinds of sectarian belonging. Put otherwise, the new model for education cannot stop with the instrumental mission of learning and training for social roles. Rather, it must strive to be com-prehensive, and to seek integral improvement of individuals who must, beyond filling roles, become truly themselves.

The Leisure Era: New Opportunities

We must stress once again that individual free time or unwatched space can only lead, sooner or later, to freedom, which means consciousness and accountability, or to permissiveness with its escorts: ignorance and ir-responsibility. The second track—casual leisure—requires no substantial training, and occurs quite often now. It is superfluous to use the space in these pages to describe once again what we can read in every newspaper and see on all TV news broadcasts. The first option, which centers on se-rious and project-based leisure, demands all the concentration and energy we can muster, along with a high sense of humanistic responsibility.

For educators, this demand should be twice as high. Educators can no longer escape responsibility for complete training of their pupils' freedom; that is, for instructing on entire freedom for whole human beings. This requires a new concept of education focused on what Gonzalez-Pecotche (1957/1984) calls "the conscious process of self improvement."

Today we are at a crossroads, and a decision must be made. The choice is not between the two sterile options mentioned above, but between them and a third option, the only one that allows people to be involved in all aspects of their chaotic, open, transparent life without losing intimate humanity. This aim can be accomplished if we know how to be familiar not only with what is going on around us but also, and more importantly, with our inner selves. "When human faculties break through the barriers of internal submission, man conquers freedom of conscience, mobilizes his reason and acquires confidence in the elaboration of his judgments; a confidence that protects him against any deceit, against any mystification, wherever it may come from" (Gonzalez-Pecotche, 1968/1993, p. 86).

Who are the teachers capable of fostering the blossoming of this authentic, intimate freedom? Such teachers are masters, and "all masters are foremost masters of humanity" (Gusdorf, 1963, p. 45). By their very existence, they show us the way to be human. A master assumes the mission of guiding another person toward self-realization as a human being, toward a sort of "Promised Land" found in the person's internal world. In this world we find peace, because we find ourselves. Leisure time invites us to enter this world, even if not always in a conscious manner.

Nevertheless, the master must take care not to flatten the peaks of life, nor reduce its horizons. For in every space and among the folds of life, a person can find critical elements in which the deep, unique self is revealed. Though life is the experimental path where battles are fought, where one wins or loses, it is also the place where the human spirit is truly forged (Gonzalez-Pecotche, 1968/1993).

While the role of masters is to accompany the child in this vital undertaking, they must try to avoid placing themselves between the child and the larger world, or between the child and his or her own self. In other words, from a very young age, children can be shown how to live with their true selves, rather than with a self that reflects only the troubled desires of those around them.

Seeing requires one to choose to observe a certain object, and this requires that observers come prepared with an internal space that allows them to receive the observed object. Seeing thus requires that people first see themselves to enable their whole self to be present in their intimate relationship with life. Contrary to the usual tendency to pull individuals outside themselves so they can take up various instrumental roles in the wider society (with the risk that they will lose themselves there), it is incumbent on the master to invite these individuals to view their own internal world. Above all, it is critical for the master to give one a clear sense about one's relationship with oneself; that is, to cultivate one's internal faculties (Gonzalez-Pecotche, 1957/1984). To cultivate these faculties is to find the kind of self-fulfillment, said earlier to be the most profound reward for pursuing serious and project-based leisure.

If life is not stuck in the gray torpor of inertia, it becomes real life, flowing through time, inviting people to define themselves in a dynamic and vital relationship. We can see life when we take care to contemplate it. We can see life when the dawn has risen in our consciousness, thanks to the light of our thoughts. Thus, only when we think in a conscious fashion, can we sense the harmonious, affirming palpitations of life.

However, to think consciously supposes that we have penetrated the world of thoughts, that we have acquired a palpable knowledge of their nature, and of their strength. To be aware in the world means that we have been exposed not only to a circumstantial world that tends to impose itself on our understanding as a unique world, but also to a transcendent world in which its echoes become increasingly clear within our internal world. Here the concepts are developed in our consciousness, which is a source of light that becomes stronger with each understanding. To be aware in this world means to acquire comprehension; that is, to reach those stages in which one attains knowledge of him or herself. This is the kind of invitation, still unclear, that one feels when he is left to his own devices in new and free spaces, where he is free of pre-established schedules, and which pushes him to search for himself.

In the Era of Leisure, more than freeing up time, all of life emerges with all its strength, inviting us to initiate and be proactive, rather than just reactive. This is a life where we find true freedom, and its very infinity, as opposed to a life filled with the prescribed action of chaotic hedonism that we have labeled casual leisure. To initiate is to translate into action thoughts about ourselves; to react means to be carried away by the surrounding hedonic wave of fun and pleasure. We have to remember that to discover freedom is nothing, the real issue is to become free; that is, to assume this freedom. Is this not the great challenge facing people when thrown into leisure?

However, only people who have the necessary resources, who know they have the potential to be the kind of person they want to be, can take on this mission. The role of education is to help them develop these resources and discover this potential. The role of education is to reconcile, at an earlier stage, the child and the child's self. The goal is to enable children to see themselves as they are, and to come to the realization that, through their own efforts, there is hope for change as well as hope for becoming the kind of person they wish to be. There is hope to realize their individual selves.

Education, inspired by the value of freedom, must offer the concepts and principles that enable individuals to conduct this dialog between their interior selves and the larger world, thereby increasing their individuality. Only this individuality can create an authentic relationship with life that will be fuller and richer in its content than before, because this life delves deeper, far deeper, than appearances.

People, in the perpetual agitation that appears to be the movement of life, allow themselves to be distracted from themselves. Thus they let this valuable time, which has only now been released, pass and disappear as just another part of life. "Time does not get lost, but rather the life of one who wastes time gets lost" (Gonzalez-Pecotche, 1976, p. 20). To allow ourselves to be swallowed up by the turbulent river of daily life is to submerge our lives in a small niche that, these days, is popularly said "to be in," but which actually means "to be out of ourselves."

However, people who strive to realize their freedom must begin by tearing down the curtains separating them from their internal world. This world is the world of thoughts before they are expressed, the world of feelings, the world of movements and acts of the will that move toward the main objective of life that is the realization of maximal self-fulfillment (Gonzalez-Pecotche, 1956). Gonzalez-Pecotche emphasizes, in particular, the importance of inner horizons, in which everything the individual sees and undergoes is reflected. To truly understand what we observe outside ourselves, we "must remain aware of what occurs within us." We need to improve our flexibility so that we can move instantaneously from the internal to the external world, move between the world of facts and deeds, between the world of thoughts that are potential acts and the concepts and principles, which we continually elaborate.

Those who govern have always feared that the people whom they rule will "find themselves" in the intimacy of their personal thoughts. The goal of education in the new Era will be to become familiar with this same intimacy of personal thoughts. Above and beyond the "wars of liberation" that occur outside of ourselves, we have to battle against imprisonment of our selves in the collective ideas that conquer our minds. This battle against the conqueror who usurps our internal sovereignty is a personal battle in which the only weapon is consciousness. If it is true that "the knife is useless against the spirit," then the dark thoughts will quickly succeed in shading our understanding and weakening all our faculties.

To realize our internal liberation is to cease being resigned to think and feel like "everyman." We must therefore go to the essence in order to know ourselves and, ultimately, to know in general. Just like darkness melts away in the face of light, so ignorance fades as consciousness expands.

One slowly becomes oneself, a personal state achieved through consciousness rather than by some instant mutation. Let us not forget that both the end of the working world and that of obligations lead to a state of falsity. Do we not see the masses who have won free time, only to be happily swallowed up; where to "live more" simply means "to consume more"?

Nevertheless, people are not what they eat and buy, but rather they are what they think. They are either the sum of their thoughts or simply the victims of passing thoughts. "Man is simply a reed—the weakest in nature; however, he is a thinking reed. . . . All of our dignity consists thus of our thoughts. Here we are supposedly revealed. . . . We must, therefore, work hard in order to think well. . ." (Pascal, 1670/1972, Pensées, no. 347). This is Pascal's brilliant message, and we know what happened to it. His fate was that of all transcendent elements that fall into the hands of superficiality: sad degeneration.

To hold thoughts in our lives that are unquestioned is to not think. "I think therefore I am," declared Descartes, by which he meant that to think consciously means to be more. To think in a conscious manner means to grow. To be aware means to be present inside ourselves.

I can comprehend and actualize my self only if I belong to myself. However, I do not belong to myself when "occupied," or trapped, by thoughts alien to my free will. That will, which has become the will of the will, takes the form of perseverance. It nurtures all objectives, but primarily the higher existential objectives, which, like any creation, requires cohesion and continuity to preserve their freshness and the vitality of the initial inspiration. Note that this is one of the six characteristics of serious leisure (see chapter 1).

Pecotche (1953) proposes a strategic plan by which we can take back possession of ourselves; that is, to conquer anew the authority of our thoughts. It is necessary to reorganize, in a clear hierarchy, all our thoughts. Presiding over all these thoughts must be the thought whose role is to ensure that the individual will do his or her utmost to grow and become more, doing so until this person ultimately becomes himself or herself. This thought is the one that reminds us that to be worthy of existence, it is not sufficient to survive; rather, we must extract the meaning of existence. The whole of our authentic existence is excited by wonder each time it meets and identifies even the smallest ray of light, even the smallest grain of truth. This is the authentic cry of liberty.

To be free is to divest one's mental space of all thoughts that encumber and block the vital forces of life. Yet how can we expect it to be easy to carry our lives, when so many people have a tendency to struggle under the great burden of useless thoughts? While it is true that doing this is essentially invisible to others, as it is focused entirely within ourselves. Our steps are the fruits of our thoughts, not the results of the current of life. Thus our visible deeds, when an expression of our deeper actions, will be stronger as our internal action becomes more intense. In the slow rise of humankind to self-knowledge, we will have to walk endlessly and alone on a path leading from learning to understanding, from understanding to knowledge, from knowledge to conscious experience, and then to begin the cycle once again and repeat it forever.

However, we are not discussing routine repetition during which life fades, being submerged into unconsciousness and inertia. To live unconsciously means to offer ourselves as victims to physical deterioration and superficial thoughts. To choose to be free is to choose to be aware of a constructive dialog with the world and to receive its infinite elements that can help strengthen and develop the person. "Every day is like a pearl that we string onto the necklace of life. How many people string stones instead, and are then forced to walk with these crushing weights" (Gonzalez-Pecotche, 1978, p. 50) Each day can give us our heritage, one that we have created; a heritage that enriches the future without burdening it.

The past is not just another pile of souvenirs that encumbers our memory and dims the present. Rather, the past is more than the sum of all the events within it, or else it is nothing. The past must enlighten the present and clarify the future, but not by way of glittering events, of which it appears we were a part. Rather the past is the sum of the knowledge we have extracted from our lived experiences. The present, as their link, becomes the fruit of the past and the seed of the future.

Projected into the space of free time, the individual must choose either to be more each time or to be someone else each time. To be, which springs from consciousness, can be the essence of the revealed self or the receptacle of all the alluvium that has collected from the hazards of existence.

In other words, the center of activity must move inward from outside. Instead of reacting to events animated by autonomous thoughts lying within oneself, action will occur that results from the conscious choice of thoughts that the individual has decided to develop. Here action emanates from being. Yet everything is found here: glittering appearances (they may promise joy or fear; some are false and always changing and ephemeral) and deep reality. The appearances attract man only to distract him; the reality waits patiently for when the person's view is ripe.

Each instance of consciousness signifies that we are accompanied by the essence of all we have learned, all we have understood, all we have realized. The more we learn, understand, and realize, the more we become ourselves. Thus people, when they transform each replica of their enriching dialog with life into knowledge, their energy reserves increase and grow. Like all things in the universe, individuals change; either they evolve and blossom, or they dry up and deteriorate.

If humankind has the privilege of sight, it also has the responsibility not to reduce itself to walking in the twilight and the responsibility to avoid following artificial lights showing a way it has not chosen. Humankind must assume this freedom, and it must choose its own way. Life is only revealed to man in the course of life.

Conclusion

The world of leisure is, from this perspective, the privileged space in which to realize this higher training. Moreover, only someone who has already bravely walked through this process may consider guiding another person along the path. The educator, according to Gonzalez-Pecotche, is one who first learns and then teaches. We are talking about learning, the goal of which is to encourage students to extract, day after day, those elements that are part of every life experience and that reveal the essence of existence. Education, as such, is internal preparation of the individual; that is, of each individual.

The time has come for education to dedicate itself to its proper objective: to accept people as they are now, and to invite them to undertake the journey of conscious improvement. This means encouraging them to think and assisting them to find the necessary knowledge to realize themselves. The supreme aim of education must be to create a culture of knowing gained through experience. We are not talking about static knowledge, but rather about dynamic knowledge, which develops at the rate of personal growth. It is an ongoing process that occurs beyond school walls and also in all the dimensions of life's multiple manifestations.

From this perspective, everything stems from, and leads to, consciousness. This is the starting point, beginning at the moment we sense the existence of the internal world and the transcendental world that echoes inside this world. This is the point at which an experience is distilled and becomes knowledge. And this is the point of arrival, where we can see our thoughts within ourselves and can observe "with integrity, serenity and courage" the horizons of existence.

To hold consciousness in a state of alertness in order to realize personal growth, is a process leading toward greater humanity. Herein lies the essence of the educational act. To teach is primarily to encourage students to move toward knowledge that is more than mere information and to enable them to advance into deeper levels of consciousness. This is an awareness that is integrated into the individual's present, enabling him or her to continually be more. Thus, one can walk within the leisure sphere, rather than being thrown into it.

In this sense to teach is to create. At each step in the spiral of development, life is more than the events within it. The role of teacher is, therefore, to invite students to transcend their reductive egocentrism in order to find their real selves, and to open authentic relationships with a range of life's manifestations. To this end, students must learn how to observe, visualize, and act – in sum, to think. In this new Era of Leisure we look further: we are talking about lifelong learning students.

In this new Era of Leisure, we have plenty of time for this. But do we have ourselves? That is also the question.

References

Aragon, L., (1946). *Il n'y a pas d'amour heureux in La Diane Française*. Retrieved October 15, 2007, from http://www.feelingsurfer.net/garp/poesie/Aragon.Amour.html

Beck, U. and Beck-Gernsheim, E. (1996). Individualisation and "precarious freedoms": Perspectives and controversies of a subject-oriented sociology. In P. Heelas, S. Lash, and P. Morris (Eds.), *Detraditionalization: Critical reflections on authority and identity*. Oxford, England: Blackwell.

Bergson, H. (1913/1927). *L'Energie spirituelle*. Paris: P.U.F.

Brightbill, C. (1961). *Man and leisure*. Englewood Cliffs, NJ: Prentice-Hall.

Buber, M., (1925/1980). *Relationship and mystery, man and his attitude in the world*. Jerusalem: Mossad Bialik.

Cachin, F., Rishel, J. (1995). *Cezanne*. Paris: Galeries Nationales du Grand Palais.

Dumazedier, J. (1988). *Révolution culturelle du temps libre*. Paris: Editions Méridiens-Klincksieck.

Focillon, H. (1943). *Vie et formes*. Paris: P.U.F.

Fromm, E. (1941). *Escape from freedom*. New York: Rinehart.

Gonzalez-Pecotche, C. (1951/1978). *Introducción al conocimiento logosófico*. Sao Paulo, Brazil: Editora Logosófica.

Gonzalez-Pecotche, C. B. (1956). *Exégesis logosófica*. Buenos Aires: Editorial Ser.

Gonzalez-Pecotche, C. B. (1957/1984). *Logosofia, ciencia y método*. Sao Paulo, Brazil: Editora Logosófica.

Gonzalez-Pecotche, C. B. (1968/1993). *El espíritu*. Sao Paulo, Brazil: Editora Logosófica.

Gonzalez-Pecotche, C. B. (1976). *Pensamientos I*. Buenos Aires: Editorial Ser.

Gonzalez-Pecotche, C. B. (1978). *Pensamientos II*. Buenos Aires: Editorial Ser.

Gusdorf, G., (1963). *Pourquoi des professeurs?* Paris: Bibliothèque Scientifique, Editions Payot.

Laloup, J. (1969). *Le temps du loisir*. Paris: Editions Casterman.

Nietzsche. F. (1887/1985) *La généalogie de la morale*. Paris: Editions Gallimard.

Pascal, Blaise, (1670/1972). *Pensées*. Paris: Le Livre de Poche.

Sartre, J. P. (1943). *L'Etre et le néant*. Paris: Editions Gallimard.

Chapter Four
Educating for Leisure
by Atara Sivan

Introduction

Educating for leisure has been widely acknowledged as an emerging need for enhancing people's quality of life. Underpinning this need are global changes in working patterns and an increase in people's free time, along with other factors such as increased unemployment rates and the misuse or abuse of leisure. The advocacy for leisure education also is derived from the notion that leisure is a basic human right that is linked to human development. If individuals have the right for leisure and leisure contributes to human development, it is essential that individuals and societies have the chance to be educated for leisure. What does educating for leisure entail? How and to what extent does it demonstrate the relationship between leisure and education, both of which are major domains of people's lives and are yet perceived as contrasting? What are the main issues to be considered when educating for leisure? Who should be undertaking this role? How and where is it implemented? Those are some of the questions that the present chapter addresses.

Educating for Leisure – Education and/or Leisure?

To educate for leisure indicates bringing together two major domains of life: namely education and leisure. The roles of these two domains have been identified as significant to human development. Thus, for example, The Convention on the Human Rights of the Child published by the United Nations (1989) stated the right of a child to an education and the right of the child "to rest and leisure, to engage in play and recreational activities appropriate to the age of the child." (p. 9). With this underlying assertion, it is of high significance to examine the relationship between leisure and education. Some of the questions that arise are: does education for leisure imply a formal process through which people study how to use their leisure time? Alternatively, does it imply that during leisure time people will become more educated? Can leisure and education complement each other in undertaking the role of educating for leisure?

An examination of the roles of leisure and education (Sivan, 2006) highlights a perceived contradiction between those two domains. This contradiction is derived from the association of education with schools, which, as social institutions, carry the functions of developing academic competence, transmitting specialized knowledge, and preparing for the workplace. Furthermore, the experience of schooling is structured, time-bound, content-oriented, and teacher and occupation-directed (Ellis, Cogan, and Howey, 1991), which does not seem to be in line with the experience of leisure. Unlike schooling, however, education is lifelong, open-ended, self-directed, can be formal and informal, and can be undertaken anywhere. It is "the sum total of one's learning experiences during a lifetime – not just organized in schools, but all learning experiences" (Ellis, Cogan, and Howey, 1991). This implies that education can also be undertaken within the leisure domain.

Leisure scholars have highlighted the interrelation between leisure and education. Some grounded it on the centrality of leisure in people's lives and the need to attend to leisure through education (Bender, Brannan, and Verhoven, 1984). Some have grounded the relationship in the learning process, which is lifelong and ubiquitous and for which leisure is a good context for exploration and enhancement (Brightbill and Mobley, 1977; Roberts 1983; Sivan, 2003). Other scholars have based the relationship between leisure and education in the philosophy of education, which encompasses preparation for leisure as one of its aims, as well as the provision of learning activities, including leisure characteristics (Parker, 1979). The latter implies that leisure can be experienced within the process of education.

The above examination indicates that despite the perceived contradiction between leisure and education, these two domains are rather complementary. It is in their roles and through the process of learning that these two domains are interrelated. These profound relationships between leisure and education serve as the solid foundation for leisure education.

Defining Leisure Education

There is no one definition of leisure education. In general terms, it has been referred to as a lifelong process through which people can better understand themselves and the role of leisure in their life and act upon this understanding to bring about desirable changes to their use of leisure. Leisure education aims to foster the development of values, attitudes, skills, and knowledge relevant to leisure so as to enhance the quality of people's lives.

Leisure education has been regarded as a developmental process (Mundy, 1998; Kleiber, 2001) which has great potential for the individual. It is through that process that people get to know themselves, their abilities, talents, and interests (Brightbill and Mobley, 1977). Moreover, they develop a sense of freedom, enjoyment, and self-worth; experience personal growth; and can discover their talents and potential (Bender, Brannan, and Verhoven, 1984). People also further develop personal values, individual goals and objectives, self-confidence and self-esteem skills, knowledge, competencies (Hayes, 1977), and self-determination (Dattilo and Williams, 1991). Other personal benefits of leisure education include the enhancement of self-initiative and self-reliance, and the increased ability and responsibility in time planning (Fache, 1995).

Alongside the personal benefits, which are highly emphasized, there are also societal gains to education for leisure. The aim of the process is to shape the environment so as to enable people to use their leisure in a creative and rewarding way without depending on organized resources (Brightbill and Mobley, 1977). Through this process, people can develop understanding not only of themselves and leisure, but also of the relationship between leisure, their lifestyles, and society. (Mundy, 1998). Lastly, leisure education aims at the encouragement of social contact and integration in networks of friends (Fache, 1995).

The personal and societal aims of leisure education are well-illustrated in a series of position statements on leisure education that were drafted in recent years. Apart from the potential contribution of leisure education to the individual, these position statements call for the implementation of leisure education as a mechanism for community development, as a way to care for populations with special needs through inclusive approach, and as a preventive measure for youth-at-risk (Ruskin and Sivan, 2002).

In a broader sense, leisure education is part of the socialization process. Mannel and Klieber (1997) distinguish between socialization "into" and socialization "through" leisure. While socialization through leisure emphasizes the significant role of leisure as a valuable resource for personal, societal, and cultural development, socialization into leisure refers to the process through which children acquire the aspects that affect their leisure choices, behavior, and experiences. Leisure education can be viewed as a practical component of socialization into leisure, which according to Mannel and Klieber involves four influential socialization agents: family, peer-group, schools, and the mass media. Being a multifaceted, developmental, and lifelong process, which aims at both individuals and society, the process of leisure education necessitates the involvement of different systems in people's lives.

Multi-system Approach to Leisure Education

Childhood and youth socialization plays a crucial role in people's development. Specifically to leisure, childhood and youth experiences affect people's leisure choices and experiences as adults (Roberts, 1999). It is therefore essential to attend to aspects of child development when educating for leisure. The process of leisure education pertains to both individuals and the society and involves several socialization agents with which individuals interact. It is within this context that the developmental settings of children and the interaction between them and the environment are to be examined. Of particular relevance to such an examination is Bronfenbrenner's (1979, 1989) ecological systems theory and its contextual elements. According to Bronfenbrenner (1979, 1989), when studying child development, one must examine the child's immediate environment as well as the interaction of the larger environment. The child's environment consists of five ecological subsystems and various structures. The interaction of structures within each subsystem and between subsystems is detrimental to the child's development. All subsystems of the environment influence each other; and children affect, and are affected by the behavior of those surrounding them.

The closest subsystem of the child's environment is the microsystem which consists of those with whom the child has a direct contact. This includes families, classrooms, peers, clubs, neighborhood, and childcare environments. The second subsystem—the mesosystem—provides the connection between the structures and role players in the microsystem. In the mesosystem, there is an interaction between the child's family, school, and peer groups, as well as between other key people that are closest to the child. The mesoystem consists of relationships, and as such it facilitates the child's development. The third level—the exosystem—includes the larger circle of the social system in which the child does not have a direct involvement, but is affected as a result of its interaction with the other subsystems. The fourth subsystem—the macrosystem—consists of cultural aspects, such as values, customs, and laws; it regulates the other three previously-named subsystems. The fifth subsystem—the chronosystem—adds the dimension of time and consists of the external and internal changes in children's lives that lead to their reaction to environmental changes.

Bronfenbrenner's ecological systems theory provides a good conceptual framework for examining the process of leisure education. Five core issues are derived from such an examination. The first and perhaps the most significant issue relates to school. Even though school provides relationships secondary to those provided at home, the amount of time children spend at school adds weight to the relationship developed there and to their influence. According to Bronfenbrenner, the instability of the modern family can be destructive to the child's development. Therefore, the role of schools and teachers is to support the primary relationship of children by providing the affirmation they search for. Gaining this affirmation from the third party relationship can develop the skills necessary for children's primary relationships. Such a disposition highlights the role of school as a socialization agent and the importance of home-school collaboration for the betterment of the child. In view of the interrelationship between leisure and education, the increased role of schools, and the bi-directional relationship of children and their closest environment, the above implies that educating for leisure in schools can have an impact on both the children's and their families' leisure and quality of life.

The second issue refers to the role of peers. Peer-group is one of the microsystems in which social and cultural learning takes place. It is within the leisure settings that peer-groups and youth culture are constructed. With their interests, adolescents have become a dominant part in the commercial marketplace. Peer-group has an impact on leisure patterns of adolescents. Studies on adolescent leisure highlight their involvement in social and expressive activities, which are undertaken with their peers (Sivan, 2000). Positive associations were found between peer orientation and actual and preferred leisure activities and participation,especially social and physical activities (Ng, 1987). The significant role of leisure in adolescents' lives and the effect of the peer-group are important aspects that may affect the other microsystems in their lives. These are important features to be considered when implementing leisure education to youth in terms of the context, strategies employed, and personnel involved.

The third issue refers to the wider subsystems in the child's life. Although the community and the society and its culture are part of the exo- and macrosystems in which the child does not function directly, their role should not be underestimated. The community and society at large provide contexts, resources, and values within which the bi-directional relationship between children and adults are developed and maintained. When referring to the area of leisure and the aims of leisure education, this implies that the development of leisure values and attitudes could be best utilized while involving different structures within the community.

Lastly, the impact of globalization as part of the macrosystem is to be considered as well. Globalization applies to the whole range of social relationships provided by cultural, economic, and political networks and intensive flows and interactions. Drawing on Bronfenbrenner's ecological systems theory, global changes may affect the bi-directional influences of the child. Specifically to leisure education, these global changes are highly related to the growing role of mass media as a socialization agent into leisure. Studies have indicated that most popular leisure activities involve the use of mass media (Sivan, 2000) and that the media has a wide range of effects on child and adolescent lives (Strasburger, 2005; Escobar-Chaves, Tortolero, Markham, Low, Eitel, and Thickstun, 2005). The leisure education process needs to acknowledge the growing impact of mass media in shaping children's and adolescents' values, attitudes, and leisure behaviors.

The above issues are pertinent to education for leisure in that they highlight the multiple systems that affect human development. Important microsystems such as the family, school, and peer-groups serve as contexts for learning. They are also recognized as socialization agents into leisure and may carry various values, attitudes, and appreciations related to leisure. To educate for leisure calls for the need to identify the potential of these contexts for leisure education, the ways through which this potential could be best utilized, and to recognize the possible changes these contexts may have on one another with the aim of facilitating human development and enhancing people's quality of life.

The Role of Schools in Educating for Leisure

As a major socializing agent within the society, schools play a significant role in the socialization process. In addition to teaching young people intellectual and technical skills, schools also teach them cultural values and attitudes which prepare them for their roles as adults. The significant role of schools in educating for leisure has been long recognized. In the early sixties, Kraus asserted in his book *Recreation and the Schools* (1964) that school is the most important agent for leisure education outside the family unit. He suggested a wide range of strategies to raise students' awareness of the importance of leisure in their lives and to develop their skills for participation in leisure activities. He further indicated the importance of providing practical experiences for students to participate in leisure activities, and the need for cooperation between school and other community agencies. Similar views of the vital responsibility of the school in educating for leisure and the need for integration and cooperation with public recreation agencies were expressed during the seventies and eighties (Corbin and Taits, 1973; Weiskopf, 1982). Ruskin (1984) indicated the potential contribution of school subjects to the development of students' intellectual, aesthetic, and physical development, which can be further nurtured in their leisure activities. One of the major arguments raised by Brightbill and Mobley (1977) for the important role of school in the process of leisure education is its being the primary institution of education. When comparing the school with the family in terms of the duty of educating for leisure, they asserted that this duty devolves heavily on schools. It derives from the fact that parents do not spend as much time with their children as their parents did with them, and thus, parents are not equipped to prepare their children for leisure. Special attention has been given to the role of school in leisure education for the adolescents, highlighting their provision of social space for the development of important roles in adolescents' lives (Parker, 1979; Kelly, 1996). Mundy and Odum (1979) stressed the need to regard the school's role in leisure education not as a complementary goal to the vocational goal, but as a goal in and of itself.

Whereas the call for schools to undertake leisure education was mainly made in the U.S. a couple of decades ago, the last decade has seen a growing international recognition of the school as a socializing agent for leisure. This can be attributed to the growing recognition of the significant role of leisure and of the need for schools to provide an all-around education. The international trend towards lifelong learning has resulted in a growing number of countries deciding to include the need to educate for leisure in their statement of educational aims. Apart from appearing in official governments' educational statements of school aims, the role of school in educating for leisure has been highlighted by leisure scholars and professionals (Sivan and Ruskin, 2000).

Support for the role of school in educating for leisure can be further found in a study among students and teachers which aimed to solicit their views on leisure education and the school system (Sivan, 1995, 1996, 1997). Results indicated that the majority of both students and teachers perceived leisure education as helping people to develop favorable attitudes towards their leisure time, enabling them to discover what leisure means to them, and helping them to identify their own skills and abilities that they can use in their leisure activities. In addition, leisure education has been perceived as helping people to choose leisure activities that meet their own needs and interests as well as helping people to learn basic physical, social, and creative skills through which they can increase their options and directions of leisure involvement.

When referring to their own schools, the majority of both populations stated that leisure education should be an integral part of their school curriculum. In their view, school programs should include teaching the knowledge of leisure; helping students to understand the meaning of leisure; and developing of leisure skills, values, and favorable attitudes towards leisure. They further maintained that schools should educate for leisure to a much greater extent than they have been doing, viewing cooperation with other community agencies, student involvement in leisure experiences, and social affairs in the community as successful channels for implementing leisure education. The areas of extracurricular activities, civic education, homeroom period, and special social activities were chosen as the best opportunities for undertaking leisure education within the school.

Framework for Leisure Education in Schools

The aim of leisure education can best be translated into practice by linking it to the educational objectives of the school system and tying it to the cultural context of society. Educating for leisure within the school involves the process of curriculum implementation, which translates plans into actions (Oliva, 1997) and necessitates the involvement of teachers, students, and other personnel, such as administrators, supervisors, parents, and other members of the community (Doll, 1996). The process can include the organization of the curriculum in a way that considers its depth and breadth.

The traditional curriculum has been criticized for not fully meeting the need to take into account students' interests and issues related to their personal and social development. Introducing a leisure education curriculum is one way to attend to this need, by infusing an area which is highly relevant to students' lives and is of growing interest in many countries. One of the ways to do this is through transdisciplinary integration in which "the curriculum is designed so that it focuses on broad learning experiences or on important problems or issues" (Morris, 1995, p. 77). While designing the curriculum on the key concept or social problem, its content is selected in a way that helps students to analyze and shed more light on the problem. Furthermore, it requires the involvement and input of a wide range of teachers so as to infuse the topic to as many areas as possible and in a way that is related to the subject taught. It further requires cooperation between teachers so that students would feel the coherence of the experiences and the link between them.

Domains Under Consideration

Both the cognitive and affective domains of development should be considered for best implementation of leisure education within school systems. The development of the cognitive domain can be achieved by increasing the individual's knowledge relevant to leisure. This consists of familiarity with a variety of leisure resources and activities as well as with the cultural heritage of society. It includes developing an awareness of the role of leisure in the individual's life and in society as a whole as well as exposing students to the way that creativity differs between communities and lifestyles. In order to facilitate the individuals' needs and inclinations in this area, students should also become more familiar with criteria for choosing and evaluating possibilities for their leisure activities. As part of this process, individuals should also be made aware of the hazards of pursuing leisure activities, which may be harmful when being overused or abused.

The affective domain of development can be attended to by fostering positive attitudes towards the use of leisure. The individuals' values and feelings underlying their preference of certain leisure activities to others can be explored through experiential learning of a range of leisure activities which could also establish a basis for developing future hobbies. Channels for experiencing relaxation techniques for people's own health promotion can be provided, as well as opportunities for carrying out volunteer and cooperative activities oriented toward sharing and helping the community.

Pedagogical Channels and Approaches

Schools can offer various formal and informal channels for implementing leisure education so as to contribute to the development of individuals. Using the formal channels implies the incorporation of leisure education into a variety of subjects and learning activities. Each subject has the potential to contribute to the achievement of the leisure education aim and objectives. Leisure education can be integrated into the regular curriculum, which aims to attend to the cognitive and affective domains of student development. Such learning can take place both in and out of the classroom. Special supporting activities, through which the students are exposed to a variety of leisure experiences, could be planned and organized in conjunction with the existing study units. These can include field trips, special projects involving the community, talks, and other creative examples which exist within the school-related context.

Informal frameworks are important channels for educating for leisure. Their unique characteristics provide an enjoyable context for developing necessary skills and fostering positive attitudes towards leisure. Some of the principles to be employed while utilizing these frameworks include trial and error, modeling, participation based on freedom of choice, structural flexibility, and involvement with the community outside of school. These are some of the basic dimensions of informal education coined by Kahana (1974). When implementing leisure education, students should be given the chance to try various activities without risking any penalty for bad performance. In order to apply the principle of freedom of choice, a variety of activities should be offered to the students. After trying several activities in a supportive environment, students can make an informed decision as to the activity in which they would like to be engaged. This would tend to increase their commitment to participation.

It is recommended that leisure education be based on experiential and creative learning without the need to measure the achievement of the learners. The process should not be confined to the classroom or the school setting and should involve other agents within the community. Furthermore, leisure education could be incorporated into ongoing activities that are part of the curriculum such as trips, parties, school breaks, and special event days.

When implementing leisure education in schools, it would be beneficial to involve teachers and coordinators whose area is highly relevant to this process. At later stages, the process could include classroom and school coordinators, teachers, and counselors. All those involved in the process should play the role of facilitators.

School-Home Collaboration

The aforementioned framework for leisure education in schools relates mainly to activities undertaken within school settings. Drawing on Bronfenbrenner's ecological systems theory, the collaboration between schools and family is of high value to a child's development. To best utilize the process of leisure education, it is beneficial to maintain school-home collaboration. Whereas the contribution of parent involvement in child's schooling has been highly acknowledged, especially in terms of the child's academic achievement (Hickman, Greenwood, and Miller, 1995), less attention has been given to the effect on the child's social and personal development that goes beyond the academic sphere. To that end, the leisure domain is a significant area, and it is precisely here that leisure education can fill the gap. This can be employed through different channels, ranging from involvement of parents in class activities, in project-based learning undertaken by the students, through community-based activities which involve families, to parent education programs.

School-Peer Relationships

Another significant aspect to be considered is school-peer relationships. As a social institution, school has the function of promoting social and group relationships. It is within a school's role to provide the learning of socially appropriate patterns of interpersonal relationships (Ellis, Cogan, and Howey, 1991). To achieve this function, it is important to provide social experience and flexible settings that can enhance group relationships. These do not need to be confined to the classroom and formal learning and are to follow the aforementioned principles of informal education. Some settings and experiences that have been suggested include extended learning days and active recreational school recesses. The extended learning day integrates the formal educational program with the enrichment of leisure program, elective leisure programs, social activities programs, and independent study. The program includes many hobbies and allows the pupil freedom of choice among different options. Active recreational school recesses use this time to involve the pupils in recreation through a variety of freely chosen informal activities. Other options include school trips and outings which are used for enrichment experiences in and for the outdoors and which can also be utilized to enhance students' knowledge of their community resources for leisure involvement (Sivan and Ruskin, 1997; Ruskin and Sivan, 2002).

The role of peers is to be considered in any offering of leisure education initiatives, especially during adolescence. Practically, this implies taking into account youth development issues and recognizing the importance of group-based settings as a way to motivate students to participate in activities. Of high relevance are the positive youth development principles and the suggested environments for their promotion (Eccles and Appleton Gootman, 2002). These include the provision of opportunities for adolescents to develop positive social values, skills, and a sense of self-efficacy; to take on leadership roles; and to contribute to their community. These principles have been applied in recreation settings for youth (Witt and Crompton, 2003). It would be useful to integrate them into the process of leisure education in schools while involving the family and other community agencies.

Media Education

It is essential that leisure education in schools would include various forms of media education. Defined as "the study and analysis of mass media" (Hogan and Bar-on, 1999, p. 341), this process can enhance students' understanding of media messages, and equip them to recognize the media's effect on their lives and to make good choices about their media use. A suggested pedagogy for undertaking this process is "edutainment" in which education is undertaken through entertainment (Nahrsdedt, 2000). When translated into practice, it implies the production and provision of education and information through entertaining, media-based experiences.

Educating for Leisure – From Theory to Practice

Numerous initiatives of leisure education have been undertaken over the past few decades. These range from position statements to development and implementation of curricula and models.

Position Statements

A series of position statements was put forward over the past decade with the aim to arouse international interest and actions in terms of expanding the development of leisure education programs. These position papers include the International Charter for Leisure Education (World Leisure Commission on Education, 2000), which highlights the role of leisure education and offers strategies for its implementation in schools and within the community. It also suggests principles and strategies for preparation and training of personnel in leisure education.

This initiative was followed by numerous position papers on leisure education and community development, populations with special needs, youth-at-risk and educating for serious leisure (World Leisure Commission on Education, 2000); physical fitness, and activity in the context of leisure education (Fu and Ruskin, 2001); and the promotion of health, wellness, and leisure as major components of quality of life (Fu and Leung, 2003).

Leisure Education Curricula and Models

When it comes to actual implementation of leisure education, one can identify various curricula and models. Two curricula were developed during the late 70s in the U.S. and Canada. Leisure education curriculum was developed in 1977 as part of the Leisure Education Advancement Project (LEAP) of the National Recreation and Park Association (Zeyen et. al, 1977). The curriculum was developed to assist public schools in developing students' understanding of the role of leisure in people's lives and the wide range of meanings of leisure experiences. It further aims to help students appreciate natural resources and their relationship to leisure and quality of life, and to be able to make decisions concerning their own leisure.

Another leisure education curriculum resource was developed by Cherry and Woodburn (1978) from the Canadian Ministry of Culture and Recreation. The resource aims to facilitate teachers' implementation of leisure education in their classes. It offers five strategies to be employed by teachers while implementing leisure education in their classes. These are teachable moments; leisure incorporated; learning through recreational activity; leisure: a topic in itself; and learning: a leisure experience, the helping relationship. Underlying these strategies are four key concepts: knowledge and understanding about leisure, personal resources and skills for leisure, personal values about leisure, and positive attitudes towards leisure.

An international survey (Ruskin and Sivan, 2002) of representatives from thirty-five countries—all of whom were holding positions in the field of education—revealed that reference has been made to leisure education in some kind of official documents in most of the countries. The study further indicated that leisure education has been integrated into school curriculum in a variety of ways, mostly during recess times, extracurricular activities, special events, and outings. Related topics included traveling, sports, arts, cultural and ethnic activities, intellectual development, citizenship education, and environmental and health education.

The pedagogy involved various forms of experiential and creative learning with special events and social activities, learning through recreation activities, school clubs, outings, and community involvement being the most popular methods. Elements of leisure education were incorporated into some specific subjects such as: English language, geography, physical and health education, music, and home economics.

The most recent school-wide leisure education curriculum was developed by the Ministry of Education, Culture, and Sports of the state of Israel. The curriculum suggests a framework for schools to undertake leisure education. The target population ranges from kindergarten to twelfth-grade students. The curriculum aims "to help the individual, the family, the community, and the society to achieve a suitable quality of life and good health by using leisure time intelligently, by developing and cultivating, physical, emotional-spiritual, mental, and social aspects, each individually or combined, as they relate to the aims of education in the country and its cultural heritage" (Ruskin, 1995b, p. 13). To best achieve this aim the curriculum sets a list of operational objectives divided into three areas: knowledge, understanding, and awareness; behavior, habits, and skills; and emotions and values. The strategies offered refer to both formal and informal frameworks with the rationale that leisure education should be infused into the learning of students both inside and outside the classroom (Ruskin and Sivan, 2002).

A recently developed curriculum-based intervention entitled "Time-Wise: Learning Lifelong Leisure Skills," was implemented and evaluated among middle school adolescents in the eastern U.S. The aim of this intervention was "to promote personal development through healthy leisure engagement and prevent the onset of substance abuse and other unhealthy behavior" (p. 311). The curriculum includes six components: self-awareness of time use and the benefits associated with leisure activities, reasons for participating in free time activities, recognizing personal interests and managing boredom, the active pursuit of meaningful activity, managing free time for balance and variety, and integration of concepts (Caldwell and Baldwin, 2004).

In addition to the above school-wide curricula, various curricula components were developed for implementation by leisure educators for students with disabilities. The following three examples include various socialization agents in the students' lives. The first one entitled "school-community link" was developed for facilitation of certified therapeutic recreation specialists for school, community, and family use. The curriculum includes six units: leisure awareness, leisure resources, leisure communication skills, making decisions independently, leisure planning, and activity skill instruction (Bullock, Morris, Mahon, and Jones, 1992).

The second curriculum is of a similar type and was designed to facilitate the transition of young people with mental retardation from school to active participation in the community. It includes five components: leisure education to facilitate choice-making and independent recreation participation, leisure coaching, family and friend support, follow-up services to maintain participation in community recreation programs, and independent community leisure participation. (Dattilo and Hoge, 1995).

The third curriculum offers a wide range of strategies for promoting lifelong participation in leisure activities for people with developmental disabilities. It includes six components: philosophy of leisure education, appropriate selection of leisure activities for instruction, instruction for skill acquisition, instruction for preference and generalization, inclusive community leisure services, and home involvement in leisure education (Schleien, Meyer, Heyene, and Brandt, 1995).

The above initiatives demonstrate to a certain extent the application of a multi-system approach to educating for leisure through their involvement of various significant subsystems, such as family, school, and community.

Concluding Remark

Educating for leisure requires the consideration of various aspects related to human development, leisure, and education. This chapter highlighted the complementing relationship between leisure and education, which serves as a solid foundation for the concept and process of leisure education. Drawing on the ecological systems theory of development, the chapter calls for the adoption of a multi-system approach in undertaking this process while basing it within the school. Underlying this approach is the significant socialization role of schools, the international trend towards well-rounded and lifelong education, the growing need to support the family as primary socialization agent, and the great potential that schools have to undertake this process. Examples provided in the chapter indicate that various initiatives have been undertaken in leisure education within different settings and populations. Yet, in order to ensure the effectiveness of leisure education and utilize its potential, it is essential to implement it as a part of the school curriculum and in close collaboration with different socialization agents within the community.

References

Bender, M., Brannan, S. A., and Verhoven, P. J. (1984). *Leisure education for the handicapped: Curriculum goals, activities and resources.* San Diego, CA: College-Hill Press.

Brighbtill, C. K. and Mobley, T. (1977). *Educating for leisure-centered living* (2nd. ed.). New York: John Wiley and Sons, Inc.

Bronfenbrenner, U. (1979). *The ecology of human development: Experiments by nature and design.* Cambridge, MA: Harvard University Press.

Bronfenbrenner, U. (1989). Ecological systems theory. In R. Vasta (Ed.), *Annals of child development,* 6 (pp. 187–251). Greenwich, CT: JAI.

Bullock, C., Morris L., Mahon, M., and Jones, B. (1992). *School-community leisure link: Leisure education program curriculum guide.* Chapel Hill, NC: The Center for Recreation and Disability Studies.

Caldwell, L. L. and Baldwin, C. K. (2004). Preliminary effects of a leisure education program to promote healthy use of free time among middle school adolescents. *Journal of Leisure Research, 36*(3), 310–335.

Cherry, C. and Woodburn, B. (1978). *Leisure: A resource for educators.* Toronto, ON: Ministry of Culture and Recreation, Leisure Education Program.

Corbin, H. D. and Traits, W. J. (1973). *Education for leisure.* Englewood Cliffs, NJ: Prentice Hall.

Dattilo, J. and Williams, D. (1991). *Leisure education: Program planning, a systematic approach.* State College, PA: Venture Publishing.

Dattilo, J. and Hoge, G. (1995). *Project TRAIL: Transition through recreation and integration for life.* Athens, GA: University of Georgia.

Doll, R. C. (1996). *Curriculum improvement: Decision making and process* (9th ed.). Boston: Allyn & Bacon.

Eccles J. and Appleton Gootman, J. (Eds.). (2002). *Community programs to promote youth development.* Washington, DC: National Academy Press

Ellis, A. K., Cogan, J. J., and Howey, K. R. (1991). *Introduction to the foundations of education.* Englewood Cliffs, NJ: Prentice-Hall.

Escobar-Chaves, S. L., Tortolero, S. R., Markham, C. M., Low, B. J., Eitel, P, and Thickstun, P. (2005). Impact of the media on adolescent sexual attitudes and behaviors. *Pediatrics, 116*(1), 303-326.

Fache, W. (1995). Leisure education in community systems. In H. Ruskin and A. Sivan (Eds.), *Leisure education towards the 21st century* (pp. 51–78). Provo, UT: BYU.

Fu, F. H. and Ruskin, H. (Eds.). (2001). *Physical fitness and activity in the context of leisure education.* Hong Kong: Stephen Hui Research Centre for Physical Recreation and Wellness, Hong Kong Baptist University.

Fu, F. H. and Leung, M. (Eds.). (2003). *Health promotion, wellness and leisure: Major components of quality of life.* Hong Kong: Stephen Hui Research Centre for Physical Recreation and Wellness, Hong Kong Baptist University.

Hayes, G. A. (1977). Leisure education and recreation counselling. In A. Epperson, P. Witt, and G. Hitzhusen (Eds.), *Leisure counseling as aspect of leisure education.* (pp. 208–224). Springfiled, IL: Charles C. Thomas Publisher.

Hickman, C. W., Greenwood , G. E., and Miller, M. D. (1995). High school parent involvement: Relationships with achievement, grade level, SES, and gender. *Journal of Research and Development in Education, 28,* 125–134.

Hogan, M. and Bar-on, M. (1999). Media Education. *Pediatrics ,104,* 341–343.

Kahana, R. (1974). Guidelines for sociological analysis of informal youth organisations. *Megamot 21*(1).

Kelly, J. R. (1996). Leisure (3rd. ed.). Boston: Allyn and Bacon.

Kleiber, D. A. (2001). Developmental intervention and leisure education: A life span perspective. *World Leisure Journal, 43*(1), 4–10.

Kraus, R. G. (1964). *Recreation and the schools.* New York: The Macmillan Company.

Mannell, R. C. and Kleiber, D. A. (1997). *A social psychology of leisure.* State College, PA: Venture Publishing, Inc.

Morris, P. (1995). *The Hong Kong school curriculum, development, issues and policies* (2nd ed.). Hong Kong: Hong Kong University Press.

Mundy, J. and Odum, L. L. (1979). *Leisure education: Theory and practice.* Champaign, IL: Sagamore Publishing.

Mundy, J. (1998) *Leisure education: Theory and practice.* (2nd. ed.). Champaign, IL: Sagamore Publishing.

Nahrsdedt, W. (2000). Training personnel for free time education, concepts and direction. In A. Sivan and H. Ruskin (Eds.), *Leisure education, community development and populations with special needs* (pp. 65–74). Oxford & New York: CABI Publishing.

Ng, P. P. (1987). *Peer orientation and leisure of schooling youths in Hong Kong.* Hong Kong: The Chinese University of Hong Kong

Oliva, P. F. (1997). *Developing the curriculum* (4th. ed.). New York: Longman.

Parker, S. (1979). *The sociology of leisure*. London: George Allen and Unwin.

Roberts, K. (1983). *Youth and leisure*. London: George Allen and Unwin.

Roberts, K. (1999). *Leisure in contemporary society*. Oxford & New York: CABI Publishing.

Ruskin, H. (Ed.). (1984). Formal and informal education for leisure-centered living: Implications for educational frameworks. In H. Ruskin (Ed.), *Leisure towards a theory and a policy* (pp. 64–79). Cranbury, NJ: Associate University Presses.

Ruskin, H. (1995). *Leisure education curricula: A framework for kindergarten to grade 12*. Jerusalem: Ministry of Education, Culture and Sport.

Ruskin, H. and Sivan, A. (2002). *Leisure education in school systems*. Jerusalem: Cosell Center for Physical Education, Leisure and Health Promotion, Magness Press, The Hebrew University of Jerusalem.

Schleien, S., Meyer, L., Heyne, L., and Brandt, B. (1995). *Lifelong leisure skills and lifestyles for persons with developmental disabilities*. Baltimore: Paul H. Brookes.

Sivan, A. (1995). Schools as socializing agents for leisure: The case of Hong Kong. In H. Ruskin and A. Sivan (Eds.), *Leisure education towards the 21st century* (pp. 167–175). Provo, UT: BYU.

Sivan, A. (1996). Current Model for leisure education in educational frameworks. In F. Fu and P. C. Chan (Eds.), *Recreation, sport, culture & tourism for the 21st century* (pp. 192–202). Hong Kong: Department of Physical Education, Hong Kong Baptist University.

Sivan, A. (1997). Recent developments in leisure education research and implementation. *World Leisure & Recreation, 39*(2), 41–44.

Sivan, A. (2000). Global influence and local uniqueness: The case of adolescent leisure in Hong Kong, *World Leisure, 42*(4), 24–32.

Sivan, A. (2003). Has leisure got anything to do with learning? An exploratory study of the lifestyles of young people in Hong Kong universities. *Journal of Leisure Studies, 22*(2), 129–146.

Sivan, A., and Ruskin, H. (1997). Successful models for leisure education in Israel. *World Leisure & Recreation, 39*(2), 39–40.

Sivan, A. and Ruskin, H. (Eds.). (2000). *Leisure education, community development and populations with special needs*. Oxford & New York: CABI Publishing.

Sivan, A. (2006). Leisure and education. In C. Rojek, S. Shaw, and A. Veal (Eds.), *Handbook of leisure studies* (pp. 433–447). Hampshire, UK: Palgrave Macmillan.

Strasburger, V. C. (2005). Adolescents and the media: Why don't paediatricians and parents "get it"? *Medical Journal of Australia, 183*(8), 425–426.

United Nations (1989). *Convention on the right of the child.* Geneva: UN High Commissioner for Human Rights.

Weiskopf, D. (1982). *Recreation and leisure: Improving the quality of life.* Toronto: Allen and Bacon, Inc.

Witt, P. A. and Crompton, J. L. (2003). Positive youth development practices in recreation settings in the United States. *World Leisure 45*(2), 4–11.

World Leisure Commission on Education. (2000). *International position statements on leisure education.* Jerusalem: The Hebrew University of Jerusalem, The Cosell Center for Physical Education, Leisure and Health Promotion.

Zeyen, D., Odum, L. L., Lancaster, R. A., Fernandez, A., Tinker, S. and Verhoven, P. J. (1997). *Kangaroo kit: Leisure education curriculum.* Washington, D. C. National Recreation and Park Association.

Chapter Five
Leisure and Lifelong Learning: Childhood and Adolescence
by Corrine Spector

Introduction

Lifelong learning is a concept that provides us with keys to open new doors. In an era of change and uncertainty, we face the challenge of learning to deal with increasing freedom and the greater responsibility that this entails. Institutions no longer provide clear answers for how to raise and educate our children; thus, learning life skills becomes more important than ever. The author relates to leisure and lifelong learning from a practical, training perspective rather than a purely theoretical approach, after years of experience with young children and youth in both leisure and educational frameworks.

For young children, learning to understand the world around them by allowing them to play without guidance is insufficient. For teens, simply filling their time with activities to curb harmful tendencies does not answer their need for identity development or teach responsible use of freedom.

Leisure can be used as a framework for teaching concepts and skills that are the beginnings of lifelong learning. Indeed, even very young children are capable of understanding underlying leisure concepts such as time, choice, the importance of questioning, and more. For adolescents, leisure can teach critical lessons about helping individuals clarify who they are and how to express their uniqueness, how to orient themselves, and how to live with others. Both age groups can also learn more specific skills, such as: decisiveness, cooperation, evaluation, differentiation, and improvisation, each according to their own level.

We will consider the concept of leisure and lifelong learning as demonstrated in the following studies:
1. a two-year experiment in leisure education developed for children ages 3 to 5 (N=120) to teach orientation skills via the

language arts and exposure to various physical and social spaces.
2. a study examining the meanings and expression of leisure and serious leisure among a group of youth ages 14 to 17 (N=50).

Our interest lies in examining whether those who learn leisure skills early in life cope better with issues of freedom and responsibility in the present and throughout their lives.

Leisure as a Training Field for Free-Choice Learning and Lifelong Learning

Learning is defined as: the acquisition of a new behavior as a result of special training; an adaptive change that can be seen in the organism's behavior, and is the result of a mutual action between the organism and its environment (Sillamy, 2003, pp. 202–3).

Formal learning refers to learning skills at school, work, or in a workshop; however, it may also be organized self-learning. Informal learning includes learning for pleasure or "day-to-day learning." Free choice learning (FCL) includes the critical element of choice, meaning that knowledge must not be disconnected from one's desires; everything taught must have personal meaning for the individual. Thus, free choice learning is of great importance in learning that takes place over the course of one's whole life; more specifically, what do we choose to learn when we are not in school (Falk and Dierking, 2002).

Lifelong learning has many meanings in different contexts (e.g., cultural, political, economic), and can take place in many types of frameworks. In the "lifelong learning" concept, learning is seen as infinite and cannot be disconnected from the flow of life. Learning takes place during doing and trying, and is about overcoming our areas of discomfort. Learning is about breaking old molds and creating new ones, whereas in traditional education, the goal is often acquiring knowledge-building on the same base. Learning is examining one's heart and soul, and focusing on what one really wants and wants to know. Learning unifies the different aspects of our personality over the course of our lifetime. Ideally, lifelong learning requires both actualization of our mental and physical abilities, and the use of practical wisdom in life management.

Since this chapter's focus is on children and youth, our discussion will consider learning for personal development, rather than learning for economic reasons, as often occurs among adults.

For teachers, who are often stressed by demands of quantitative achievements, it is important to remember that learning is part of a process of development, and that this is true for all ages. Often we do not give very young children the credit they deserve; they are indeed able to choose and do things by themselves. We must try to understand why we, as teachers or parents, are often afraid of what will happen if the children choose by themselves. We must not be afraid that they will become too excited and get out of control. We must believe that they will make good choices and achieve what we think they should. When the children are older, we must not be afraid of what damage these young people might do to our society and to themselves. Most parents are worried, lest their children not live up to their potential. If all of these concerns are accurate, we must then ensure that we give children and teens the tools to deal and cope with their freedom, rather than trying to control their lives for them.

Current Conceptions of Leisure Education Among Children and Youth

We are moving towards an era in which people will increasingly need to deal with free time. It is our responsibility as educators to assist our children and youth in doing so, just as we must deal with fulfillment of young peoples' social roles on every level.

From the author's experience of the Israeli school system, the curriculum in schools is comprised of educational units in which the children take the role of "pupil" or "student," and of short breaks or recesses during which the children are meant to "take their minds off things" in order to increase their mental and physical capacity for subsequent lessons (Spector and Cohen-Gewerc, 2000). This school format is an imitation of the working life of adults, who work for extended periods, which are then punctuated by short vacations which are intended to take their minds off of their routines via some form of recreation.

School is the space of time that society provides its children as a time when they are free of the need to support themselves financially. This period can be seen as an investment in the development of the individual for the continued existence and development of society.

Furthermore, today's children are expected to live in a world that is seen by many as "the end of the work [era]" (Rifkin, 1996), and if this is the case, it would be wise to prepare them for such a future. To be "free" means to cope with an open schedule in which personal decisions are both plentiful and essential. The main challenge in this type of coping is to know how to choose channels of investment for 'free' time. A lack of direction presents one with the need to take personal responsibility for these choices.

This environment of freedom, in which the constant and known factors are becoming fewer, requires the following orientation skills: the ability to distinguish, evaluate, and determine what is 'best' from among many choices. In fact, all of these are the basis for the full realization of freedom.

The tools of leisure can be a means for training children to cope with their freedom and the resulting responsibility. Thus, this topic must be included in the school curriculum.

From this perspective, any space of "doing" in the school can become a leisure space, both in terms of the students' awareness and that of the teachers who accompany their development. In other words, the element of choice can be achieved by frequent activities in which the students have direct leisure experiences where they are invited to obtain leisure tools to help them deal with freedom, time, choice, decision, responsibility, and indirectly, by using these tools in their approach to all school (and other) activities.

This approach can be applied in any space in which there is free time, after individuals fulfill various tasks resulting from their various roles. The school can create a time in which the choices are as broad as possible, free from calculations of worth, and devoid of fixed schedules for their completion. As one student said in an interview with the researcher, "I learn the most about time when I must deal with time on my own."

Leisure Education Focus in each Age Group

The nature of leisure education is strongly related to age groups; thus, we will consider each scholastic stage as follows:

In the nursery school/kindergarten age group (ages 3–5), most time should be spent on the development of orientation skills in the space of time, and in terms of experiencing choice, while also being exposed to various physical and social spaces.

In primary school, systematic efforts should be made to develop leisure skills within a process of broadening the systematic learning commitment. Experiences with free time should take up a large space in determining how one's time is spent, focusing on the presence of the student at school.

In junior high schools, emphasis should be placed on the teens' coping with managing one's time in general, rather than only the time relating to school. Here value judgments will occur naturally, such as developing the ability to create personal priorities, in which the individual will be required to set aside some time for giving/receiving/volunteering, and for dealing with leisure and other opportunities that come his or her way, whether commercial, structured, or public.

In high school, it is necessary to deepen the learning on this topic to a level of understanding about personal coping with free time and its meanings for adult life management. One result of such a multi-year program could be that most of the students' learning will be independent in nature and the student will become an independent learner.

It is essential to translate the values we have mentioned here into educational "doing" in every field via: dealing with free time, evaluating risks and opportunities, developing an ability to discriminate between two things (e.g., good/bad, productive/wasteful, etc.), observation, contemplation, listening, asking questions, meeting oneself, reflection and initiation of self and others. Specific content can include: the legitimacy of different people/things/ideas, creativity, casual leisure, serious leisure (hobbies, amateurism, volunteering), economy of experiences, leisure education. In the author's view, leisure is a parallel discipline rather than actual educational content; thus, it is possible and important to combine the values, skills, and content of leisure in various learning areas.

Individual Age: A New Concept for a New Era

In personal communications with the editors of this book about the concept of "individual age," Cohen-Gewerc referred to it as follows: "Assuming that we realize that we must educate people to be able to undertake leisure via their own efforts, that is, by educating themselves, we must consider 1) how we can all learn to adapt to changes that occur at any age, and 2) how can children and youth recreate themselves under any circumstances, including consideration of age-related matters" (Cohen-Gewerc & Stebbins, personal communication, November 5, 2005).

As we will see in the experiment dealing with children of daycare/nursery school age (ages 3–4), the goals were indeed to teach them orientation skills that would help them adapt to changes, and also teach them how to question and think about recreation and other activities. Again, learning those skills at such an early age can only ensure that these are part of one's "toolkit" on a permanent basis. Teens who learn to recreate themselves under any circumstance will also have a better basis for dealing with the increased freedom that Western society provides. They will, of course, occupy themselves with age-relevant recreation, whether spending a good deal of time with friends and/or spending time in contemplation (both of which will help them "recreate themselves" under any circumstance). We will examine this issue further in a later section.

In a personal communication with Stebbins (2005), he stated that, "'Individual Age' means that there is an increasing emphasis on personal interests" (as opposed to collective interests). According to Beck and Beck-Gernsheim (1996), we live in an age of high individualism, expressed in significant part through the pursuit of certain mostly serious leisure activities. We must therefore ask: "How is leisure individualism expressed in the leisure of children and adolescents, if at all?" and, "What are the implications of this for leisure education?"

As we can see, leisure that is focused on the individual is essential to free choice learning, and to lifelong learning. In fact, young children are generally required to follow certain educational frameworks, and their free time may actually be quite limited in terms of choices that they make for their leisure time; they appear to be busy playing and enjoying leisure, but this is usually not the case. There is often little freedom for them to choose; they are told what to do and how to do it. Thus, it is important for leisure education to provide them with orientation skills that will ultimately allow them to choose for themselves and allow them to make more informed choices about their activities.

Among teens, we often assume that they engage in leisure activities because their friends are involved. This study, however, found that this is not completely true, as at some point young people might no longer "find themselves" in an activity they have joined because of friends, and will ultimately leave it to pursue another, even despite close friends' involvement. Most young people will then be likely to join another activity on the basis of their own interests, as their self-identity is of critical importance to them at this stage, sometimes even more than their need to belong. Ultimately, they will make new friends who are a part of this "scene," and feel that they "belong" once again while honoring their own interests.

Thus, leisure education indeed must deal with this important challenge of teaching young people to honor their own interests by attempting to deal with them on an individual basis or at least by pointing them in a direction that will lead to self-fulfillment, and also allow them to meet others who can further their particular interests.

Stebbins saw serious leisure as a central life interest among those members of society who work less and less. While he spoke of unemployed and retired populations, this is in fact also true for children and teens who do not "work" even though they may attend school during many working hours of the week.

In this study, rather than a hierarchy of preference among leisure activities, teens gave individual meaning to the importance of their leisure activities (whether defined by adults as serious or casual), showing also what Laermans noted: "what was formerly part of collective culture is now a matter of personal preference." (Stebbins, 1996).

Furthermore, the marginalization that teens feel in leisure and in life is also similar to others who live a serious leisure lifestyle, but marginalization is also something that teens are used to.

Leisure in Childhood – An Experiment in Leisure Education for Very Young Children

Generally, we refer here to childhood as ages 3 to 12. In our present reality, childhood has changed, in that the world is in many ways more "full"—of events, colors, choices, activities, and so forth. Young children must now cope with more change earlier and more frequently. Central leisure issues in childhood are: trial and experimentation, understanding the world around them, the need for belonging, freedom to choose, and taking responsibility for their choices (Erikson, 1950/1993, Piaget and Inhelder, 1969).

Let us now examine leisure education for very young children in a specific experiment. The background to this experiment was the Israeli Board of Education's desire to keep the curriculum "fresh" by implementing a few new ideas each year. Thus, an experiment on leisure education was planned and executed at a multi-disciplinary art enrichment center with three associated kindergartens (with 40 children per class). The experiment involved the children and their teachers, supervisors, and parents within the community.

Underlying Assumptions:

The field of leisure and the arts can be used as a means to help children practice life skills, making full use of their freedom and expressing their uniqueness. Hopefully, this will enable them to deal with their lives in a responsible, meaningful manner.

Goal of the experiment:

To develop orientation skills among children ages three to five via "The Language of the Arts," in physical and social realms, and in the space of time.

Definition of terms:

1. Orientation skills: Orienting oneself in an uncertain environment demands the abilities to differentiate, evaluate, improvise, cooperate, and to be decisive.
2. The language of the arts: "The arts" as an experiential place that demands active involvement and the use of one's intellect, emotions, and body.
   - Music, theatre, 3-D art, literature.
   - Here, children can explore a new order among colors, sounds, and shapes while using all of their senses.
   - Using this medium, children can learn to express their uniqueness.
3. The physical realm: The whole space of educational "doing" which becomes, for both child and educator, a space for leisure learning.
4. The social realm: The place where one individual meets another individual or several others; this requires mutuality. Different skills are needed for coping in different social situations. Each social realm has different requirements and provides unique rewards.
5. The space of time: For educators, each moment is an opportunity for encouraging the child to broaden sensitivity, increase control, support curiosity, encourage exploration, and strengthen skills.

Methods:

Prior to the experiment, leisure professionals provided sixty hours of training to the staff, supervisors, and parents of the children. During the experiment, in-depth personal interviews were held, observations were made, and individual accompaniment ("Initiation") of staff took place. Evaluation of results, beliefs, and objectives occurred on an ongoing basis, and teachers' diaries and photos were also used for documenting the experiment and results.

Results – Children:

We determined in advance that the measures of success would include seeing that children internalized the new concepts and demonstrated the new orientation skills with understanding. We used the following measures:

1. Turning a disadvantage into an advantage
   - The lunchroom in the kindergarten was small and dark. Painting and putting up pictures didn't help. We realized that eating is part of leisure culture, so we could play with it by looking at eating in different ways: A French breakfast, an outdoor picnic, the children preparing different kinds of bread and so on. This became a daily highlight for creativity over the course of the experiment.
2. Orienting oneself in different environments
   - Instead of having a "doctor's corner" in the small classroom, one boy said he would be a traveling doctor and take his doctor's bag to see his patients, wherever they were.
3. Expressing myself as a group member
   - This involved children building a project together, and playing "jazz" on pipes together in a symphony. From this, they learned that the whole is often greater than the sum of its parts.
4. Awareness of choices and the ability to choose
   - Instead of just looking at musical instruments or hearing the teacher play them, teachers asked each of the children to choose an instrument. The children then told their friends what was unique about his or her particular instrument, and this helped them understand the costs and benefits of their choice.
5. Expressing your uniqueness
   - In one example, we saw a girl presenting a play to the other children in her own way, and in her own "voice."
6. Ability to question
   - Many children wanted to present plays but had difficulty; thus we helped them ask the necessary questions: (e.g., What's the story? What should the scenery be? What will the audience like?). In the end, the children took center stage in plays and also used the world of theater as a tool for self-expression.
7. Improvising, being flexible
   - The children learned about improvisation in jazz. In a later lesson about 3-D art, when looking at a picture by Fabian (an

artist who deals with recycled materials), a 5-year old boy said "Look! Fabian improvises too!"

8. Coping with changing situations
   • The children and teacher developed a story together and every minute, the teacher made changes in the storyline to see how the children would react and what kinds of creative solutions they would come up with. They had to create environments and/or make changes to themselves to deal with the new situations.

9. Discovering various forms of leisure
   • Rather than a closed dialogue between teachers and parents about a child's leisure, we asked the children to bring something of their leisure activities from home. Many brought collections of all kinds and then began to discuss and trade amongst themselves. Their hobbies took on new dimensions of presentation, questioning, comparison, and trade decisions.

10. Meanings of time
   • We built an hourglass so the children could "see" time and know when each child's turn was finished. This way, they took control of their own time, rather than having the teacher be the judge. Another example: In the middle of a theater experience, a school bell rang nearby, and a three year-old boy said, "Listen! There's a different time outside!"

Discussion and conclusions:

Our society allows children time free of obligations so that they can play, and this is seen as an investment in the child's development as a person. In this experiment, we taught children about self-orientation in a changing world, via leisure and the arts. The goal of this intervention was to enable them to deal with their freedom in a responsible and meaningful manner.

Issues encountered during the research included:
   • The need for trust in the process and a willingness to experiment on the part of children, parents, teachers, and supervisors.
   • The need to rethink basic definitions and assumptions despite the difficulty involved. For example, What is time? Can a child of this young age decide and be responsible for his or her choices? Whose agenda is it: the teacher's or the children's?

The importance of learning that occurred face to face these issues will be discussed in terms of lifelong learning in the final section of this chapter.

Youth and Leisure in Youth – A Study of Meaning in Leisure and Serious Leisure among Youth

Today's youth must deal with greater freedom, without always being equipped with life skills that enable them to know themselves or to enjoy their freedom while also taking responsibility for it (Bilski, 2004). Often, development of these life skills is neglected by parents, schools, and/or the youth themselves. Central issues for youth in terms of leisure are: identity, meaning, freedom, choice and responsibility, creation/initiative, casual and serious leisure, and relevant leisure education for their age group (Hendry, Shucksmith, Love and Glendinning, 1993).

The need for leisure activities stands at the center of youths' existence. However, socialization agents dealing with leisure often feel the need to simply "fill up" the youths' free time, perhaps to ensure that they do not fall into harm's way. Sadly, little or no time remains for the young person to meet him or herself in such leisure situations.

This study examined the types of leisure activities among a group of 50 adolescents (from academic institutions but different backgrounds), ages 14 to 17. A qualitative approach using semistructured interviews analyzed via content analysis to understand the meanings of leisure and serious leisure from the teens' perspective.

The study examined the six distinguishing qualities of serious leisure: perseverance, a sense of "career," personal effort, benefits (self actualization/fulfillment, self-enrichment, self-expression, self-renewal/re-creation, individual and group accomplishment, enhanced self-image, social interaction and belonging, lasting physical products, and pure fun), a unique ethos, and a resulting strong personal identification with the serious leisure activity (Stebbins, 1982).

In which leisure activities do you participate?

When the subjects' activities were listed, the researcher found that each subject participated in, on average, six kinds of leisure activities simultaneously, and most participated in at least one form of what they considered serious leisure. However, upon further examination, almost half of the young peoples' leisure activities could be defined as serious. In leisure research, generally, the focus is often on the state of mind during leisure, rather than on the activities in it. That is, people choose an activity for its qualities and the experience it provides. Although work, educational studies, and maintenance-type activities are not thought of by most adults as leisure, the young people here considered them to be leisure – supporting the state-of-mind leisure theory. According to subjects, there were five types of leisure activities: liberal arts, social, sport, maintenance, and studies/work. Interestingly, similar values and benefits were found in different activities, meaning that one might gain a sense of achievement from both sports and music.

Describe your behavior patterns in leisure activities.

Rather than hearing about what they did (what, when, how often), the researcher was surprised to hear subjects discuss the meanings of their activities, which were of greater importance to them than the content. The data was categorized into eight areas: six according to Stebbins's six distinguishing qualities, and two particular to youth: escapism and choice (Rojek, 1994; Robertson, 2000-2001), and others, as follows:

1. Perseverance—objective and subjective amounts of time spent in serious leisure activities; how much "life" they've invested in doing something.
2. Career—teens occasionally saw a serious leisure activity as a potential work career and/or central life interest with progression as they continued their participation. They have the unique ability to commit deeply to an activity without paying the full price in terms of future commitment.
3. Personal effort (required for development of knowledge, training and/or skills)—teens spoke of self-directed, free choice learning and internal, external, and mixed motivations for gaining knowledge, training, and skills.
4. Escapism—escape from routine, studies, daily pressures, or escape to a space for observation or contemplation (cf., Sartre, 1943).
5. Internal or external influences—the internal or external influences on choice and the high degree of personal responsibility for their own choices. The teens had internal motivations (e.g., "I invest in my studies because I want to; I direct myself. It's important to me and I love to study. I 'decode' the material and run with it."), external, but positive, motivations (e.g., "My skating coach does the choreography for me."), and sometimes both internal

and external motivations (e.g., "My mother and I sit together and figure things out.").

6. Meaningful others—usually friends were more important than the activity. Occasionally, the activity was more important than the friends, and rarely, activities and friends were of equal importance. Surprisingly, family was often chosen for leisure and fulfilled the teens' need to strengthen family ties.

7. Moods—teens often asked whether a mood comes before an activity, or whether an activity brings about a mood. One subject said, "Once I finish writing, the page stays angry, but I feel much better!"

8. Benefits—in terms of benefits, the study found:

   • Self-enrichment—teens see self-enrichment as an addition to any leisure activity, and to one's life in general. (e.g., "I solve my personal and spiritual problems via reading. It also helps me develop my thinking abilities and questioning skills.")

   • Self-expression—a reflection of one's self which can occur in any leisure activity. Serious leisure is a space for teens to develop their thought processes and to "leave their mark"; leisure can be used as a "pipeline" to tell society their views.

   • Enhanced self-image—conditions are created in serious leisure that enable teens to become who they wish to be, physically, socially, and emotionally. (e.g., "Basketball answers my need for fitness, improves my performance, and fulfills my aspirations to be better.")

   • Lasting physical products or memorable experiences—both may be symbols of an internal process that has taken place during serious leisure. (e.g., "It's easy for me to look back at my old-fashioned sketches and see the progress that I am making all the time.")

   • A unique ethos of norms and values develops around each serious leisure activity. An individual involved in a serious leisure activity experiences a process of self-discovery, an opening of horizons, and a place for contemplation and observation of oneself. Teens may accept all, some, or none of the norms and values that come about from participation in an activity. The partial acceptance of norms and values is described in the following example: A religious girl reads stories about the secular world that are first approved by her father. She thus keeps the norms and values of reading and of her community in a unique way; as she said, "This way,

I have a window to the world, even when they try to shut us out…"

- Strong personal identification with serious leisure—resulting from all previous qualities of serious leisure. Teens begin to develop a new self-identity and related sense of pride, presenting themselves to others in terms of their serious leisure activity. As teens focus on development of their self-identity, they may "try on" several serious leisure identities; at some point, one or more serious leisure identity becomes part of their self-identity.

What is the meaning of leisure for you?

Teens defined leisure as free time before and after obligations. They did not look at the meaning of the leisure activities themselves, but rather at the meaning of leisure in general. They linked leisure with freedom and internal motivation and saw differences between free time during the school year and during vacations, in terms of choice and time use. Another important issue is teens' dissatisfaction with school and the desire for leisure education.

1. Choice— *"During my vacation, I can do what I want, when I want. Maybe I won't do anything at all, or maybe I'll do lots of things intensively."*

2. Time use— *"Free time is time in which you know you must do something important. Then it's leisure!"* Teens speak about using this time for "real doing": for exercising their unique tendencies, for giving expression to things they love, and for contemplating themselves, their future, new ideas, and the meaning of life. This contemplation seems to be especially important for youth, even if they often appear to be or report "doing nothing."

3. Teens' dissatisfaction with school and the desire for leisure education—In an online survey of 10,378 teenagers (the American National Governors Association, Janofsky, 2005), almost two-thirds said they would work harder if classes were more demanding or interesting. Fewer than two-thirds believed that their school had done a good job challenging them academically or preparing them for college, and rated effectiveness of their schools in preparing them for the future as low. One conclusion is that high school students are actually more willing to be "stretched" than we give them credit for.

This was consistent with other studies showing gaps between what students learn in high school and what they [and business people and politicians] believe is needed for the years beyond. American schools have been too slow to adapt high school curriculums to the real-life demands of college and the workplace (Janofsky, 2005).

The teens in our study also expressed a desire for leisure education within the school framework, despite their participation in serious leisure activities. Several noted that teaching them tools for dealing with their free time would allow them to make optimal use of it. One teen said, "In school, they should teach you how to manage your free time. When you have a lot of time, it's an art to know how to decide what to do, and when to do it: how not to waste your time, and how to set priorities."

Teens can also benefit from guidance in their self-directed activities; however, we must remember not to control, but to support them.

Discussion:

Leisure, and particularly serious leisure, acts as a medium between teens and the world, allowing them to try different identities, exercise their ability to choose, and think and do as they wish. It is a kind of laboratory for trial and investigation, where teens can practice roles, observe the world around them and their place in it, examine their norms and values, and try life skills without paying the full price; Here they are the ones who dictate the questions and principles in order to learn about themselves and their worlds.

Serious leisure creates opportunities for personal growth, and turns one's life into a field for lifelong learning, allowing an individual to learn and exercise a myriad of universal human abilities: taking initiative, creating/using one's imagination, taking responsibility, leading, understanding one's part in the whole, understanding costs and benefits of choices, "leaving one's mark," exercising self-discipline, searching for meaning, distinguishing between good and bad, being autonomous, practicing internal listening, taking time to observe, supporting others and volunteering, maintaining human dignity, and practicing lifelong learning.

Rather than using free time in an unfulfilling manner, it can be used for exposing teens to serious leisure, inviting a search in which there is a real chance to discover one's uniqueness. Leisure time can nourish one's development and be used as time invested meaningfully rather than time consumed thoughtlessly. Life skills developed in the realm of serious leisure are especially critical for young people in our complex age.

Conclusions: Children, Youth, and Lifelong Learning

There is a great need for teaching orientation and life skills within leisure education so that even young children will know how to cope well in physical space, in the realm of time, and in various social settings. The tools of leisure can be used to teach these skills. The child or youth must be in the center of such experiences (rather than the teacher or parent) to make such teaching most effective and true. There is often also a need to change both the physical space in which such teaching occurs, as well as the curriculum. Parents and teachers must be a part of the leisure education process, but in a supportive rather than directive role. There is a great need for interdisciplinary understanding in leisure education, and various tools in realms of art and sport may be used.

Humans are active animals; even if they are not "working," people always keep busy with activities that contribute to them in various ways that are meaningful for them. Leisure activities allow people to be autonomous, and to define their own objectives. For very young children, this begins with play that allows them to explore their worlds and find meaning in it. In this open space, beyond instrumental roles and commitments, empowerment of the individual is possible. Here, individuals of all ages win freedom and legitimacy by way of experience, learning, and self-determination, as opposed to being part of the flow of life, pulled along by circumstances.

Teens supported the "State of Mind" approach to leisure; that is, the meaning of an activity for them was more important than what they were doing. Any type of activity can bring about serious leisure benefits, depending on how people relate to what they are doing. Even watching TV can bring benefits to an individual if his or her state of mind is "serious"—that is, if he or she approaches the televised material critically or analytically.

Teens report a need to have "open time" to do nothing or for contemplation. Perhaps we can help them to develop their thinking capacity through serious leisure so that it will have some direction and progression. Serious leisure offers teens a framework both for developing their uniqueness, and for learning universal human abilities. It is therefore an excellent framework for teaching our young people.

Leisure today can often be seen as de-socialization; a meeting with oneself, rather than always a meeting with others, or simply being busy.

Leisure can also be seen as a second chance that has not been provided by the formal educational system.

Serious leisure can be the space in which individuals can develop their life skills in order to make meaningful use of their expanding freedom and to help young people (and their parents) not to be afraid of it. If people are meant to be free, then serious leisure can be a space in which a person can experience various kinds of coping with life in this age of uncertainty.

It is important to view learning as a spiral process, rather than just circles of knowledge that might be interrelated. That is, we do not want to add more closed circles, but rather understand how to develop inter-related areas of learning—areas, that with an upward movement, sweep in all of our experiences. We want to avoid the state of inertia, with its individual islands of knowledge.

The two studies presented here illustrate that lifelong learning is a process that starts at a very early stage. During this process, ideally, on-going opportunities allow us to create new ideas, and to find and express our authenticity. Sometimes this happens, not because we want it to, but rather because we must do so in order to deal with our changing reality. Lifelong learning requires us to ask: What is my central focus right now? Am I on the right course? How do I feel about the world around me? What do I need right now? What did I just learn about myself, and about others?

How does this lifelong learning create new meaning for us in our lives rather than just providing more diplomas? It is important that we not only learn more and more limited technical skills, but also that we focus on those universal human abilities that make us better, more adaptable human beings.

How do I approach life with my hands full, rather than just with low-level skills that I apply in limited situations? How do I synthesize knowledge and make new and unique use of it for my whole life, rather than just at one particular moment? To make best use of opportunities, we must know how to approach them openly, rather than being stuck and limited by our knowledge and attitudes. We must also know how to reach the essence of things in terms of their simplicity, rather than just gaining more and more complexity. We must feel comfortable enough to be brave and take chances to get further and develop.

Life is a never-ending learning experience of discovery, curiosity, wonder, and surprises. We should all have a willingness to try unusual things in depth—to jump into the eye of the storm, to fall on our faces, to do more than we expected, and to expose the truth that is encompassed within us. This is learning which allows us to commit to our deepest drives, and to the fire within us in order to attain a full and meaningful purpose. Lifelong learning is important both for developing ourselves and for giving to others: to enlighten and awaken them.

References

Beck, U. and Beck-Gernsheim, E. (2002). *Individualization: Institutionalized individualism and its social and political consequences*. London: Sage Publications.

Bilski, R. (2004). *The lure of happiness; the study of happiness—Meanings, consequences and conclusions*. Jerusalem: Carmel Publishers.

Erikson, E. H. (1950/1993). *Childhood and society*. New York: W. W. Norton & Co.

Falk, J. H. and Dierking, L. D. (2002). *Lessons without limits: How free-choice learning is transforming education*. Oxford: Alta Mira Press.

Hendry, L. B., Shucksmith, J., Love, J. G., and Glendinning, A. (1993). *Young people's leisure and lifestyles*. London: Routledge.

Janofsky, M. (2005, July 16). Students Say High Schools Let Them Down. *New York Times*. Retrieved March 20, 2006, from http://www.nytimes.com.

Piaget, J. and Inhelder, B. (1969). *The psychology of the child*. London: Rutledge & Kegan Paul Ltd.

Rifkin, J. (1996). *The end of work*. New York: Putnam & Sons.

Robertson, S. (2000–2001). A warm, safe place: An argument for youth clubs. *Youth and Policy, 70,* 71–77.

Rojek, C. (1994). *Ways of escape: Modern transformations in leisure and travel*. Lanham, MD: Rowman & Littlefield.

Sartre, J. P. (1943). *Etre et le neant* [Being and nothingness]. Paris: Edition Gallimard.

Sillamy, N. (2003). *Dictionnaire de psychologie* [Dictionary of Psychology]. Paris: Larousse.

Spector, C. (2005). *The meaning of serious leisure among various types of Israeli youth*. Unpublished master's thesis, Bar Ilan University, Ramat Gan, Israel. (Hebrew)

Spector, C. and Cohen-Gewerc, E. (2000). From education to initiation. In H. Ruskin & A. Sivan (Eds.), *Leisure education in school systems*. Jerusalem: Magnes Press-Hebrew University, pp. 121–127.

Stebbins, R. (1982). Serious leisure: A conceptual statement. *Pacific Sociological Review, 25*(2), 251–272.

Stebbins, R. A. (1996). Casual and serious leisure and post-traditional thought in the information age. *World Leisure & Recreation 38*(3), 4–11.

Chapter Six
Leisure and Lifelong Learning: Middle and Old Age
by Francis Lobo

Introduction

The purpose of this chapter is to show how leisure education and lifelong learning have the power to enhance the quality of life across the lifespan. This chapter will focus on working persons in mid-life and on older individuals after the cessation of paid employment. It takes the view that preparation for life during and after work not only assists in more satisfying lifestyles, but also helps with life balance during the life cycle. The key to optimal adjustment is through leisure, more specifically serious leisure within the disposition and framework of lifelong learning. The paper suggests ways of aging well and recommends approaches for personal development and further learning.

Lifelong Learning

Lifelong learning does not have the same connotation as recurrent education within the educational system. It reflects a more holistic view on education and recognizes learning in and from many different environments. Lifelong learning may be related to recurrent training within the education system, but it is not the same thing. Lifelong learning is life-wide and is a concept with broader scope and consequences. Lifelong learning dissolves the boundaries between education, economic, and social endeavours of individuals and groups. It may be defined as all purposeful learning activity undertaken on an ongoing basis with the aim of improving knowledge, skills, and competence (Häggström, 2002). Lifelong learning contains various forms of education and training—formal, nonformal, and informal. It is inclusive of the traditional school system from primary to tertiary level, free adult education, informal search and training, individual effort, in groups, or within the framework of social movements.

Lifelong learning has two dimensions—vertical and horizontal. The vertical dimension takes into account learning during the various periods of the life span. The horizontal dimension refers to learning of various activities concurrently during specific periods of the life span. The term life-wide is used for the horizontal dimension. Lifelong learning may be instrumental in purpose; learning to gain a professional qualification in order to secure a job is an example. Learning also refers to cultural enrichment and efforts to improve the quality of life and human development, benefits that have received international support (Longworth, 1995; Delors, 1996; OECD, 1996). This chapter focuses on the latter and does not focus on learning that leads to paid employment or certification. Instead, it deals with engagement in things that are cultural, or found in the arts, sport, and leisure pursuits. The learning of these activities is meant to provide the balance necessary for personal development, and for living a fulfilling life for the betterment of society.

The words "leisure society" were used by du Bois-Reymond (1999) to describe learners as a group. He further categorized them into four types: 1) intrinsically motivated intellectuals; 2) extrinsically motivated mass learners, as represented by modern school youth; 3) extrinsically motivated learners in continuous requalification; and 4) intrinsically motivated "trendsetters" (du Bois-Reymond, 1999). According to du Bois-Reymond (1999), although intrinsically motivated learners tend to be found in the upper end of the social structure in a learning society, different learning types cannot be strictly associated with particular social classes. Unlike extrinsically motivated learners, intrinsically motivated learners develop a strategic attitude toward learning and combine formal cultural capital with more informal experiences. During childhood, parental and social environment are of paramount importance to the development of a stable attitude toward learning. The motivation for learning of adolescents and young adults with inadequate education may be low, and they could be alienated from learning and school. Adolescents and young adults with the potential for intrinsic learning realize the personal and social advantages in allowing learning, work, and leisure time to penetrate each other. The learning society must convince all its members, including extrinsic learners and individuals in marginalized groups, that allowing this penetration of learning, work, and leisure time improves the opportunities of life.

Framework for Lifelong Learning

The Delors Report (1996) commissioned by UNESCO embraced the notion of learning throughout life. It proposed four "pillars" as foundations for learning. The document saw education as a cyclical pattern which involves studying, working, going back to study, changing jobs, semiretirement, and study. The cyclic pattern is contrasted with the traditional linear pattern of study, work, and retire, and highlights the reality of periods of nonwork discretionary time. The Delors Report supported the shift from "education for a job" to "education for a quality of life." This view, referred to by the Commissioners of UNESCO as the power "to be," emphasizes the development of "whole" human beings and the need for a balance of priorities. The balanced approach to education is reflected through what Dr. Francis Lobo, in his keynote address at the Melbourne UNESCO Conference, 1998, referred to as the intelligence of the mind, the intelligence of the hand, and the intelligence of the heart (Haw & Hughes, 1998). The skills required for learning throughout life are consistent with the "learning to do" pillar in the Delors Report. A broadening of the learning experience, rather than the mere transmission of factual knowledge, is seen to enhance learning. The idea of learning differently and the notion of learning-to-learn are in keeping with his "learning to know" pillar. The synergistic benefits of collaboration espoused by Delors is the "learning to live together" pillar. It emphasizes the contribution of diverse agencies, resulting in individual and community benefits. Such moves towards connectedness imply respecting others on the basis of equality (Haw and Hughes, 1998).

The Delors Report highlights the importance of education drawing out the "treasure" of each individual and the individual in society. Inherent in the notion of tapping the treasure within the community is that of social inclusion. If lifelong learning is considered to be an achievable goal in the twenty-first century, gaps in the comprehensive provision of education must be addressed. Nazareth (1999) shows how music-making opportunities for unemployed adults enables rediscovery of dignity of individuals. This is what Delors referred to as the "learning to be" pillar.

The Delors Report also emphasizes the importance of flexible pathways, including multiple entries and exits to educational opportunities, cooperation and exchanges, a respect for diversity, interdisciplinary approaches, making education responsive to learners' choices, a multiplicity of learning environments, and nurturing of creators who think for themselves rather than rote learners who acquire information without question.

Rationale for Lifelong Learning

The rationale for lifelong learning is multi-faceted and includes a con-nectedness between mind, body, and feeling; holding several careers during the lifespan; the changing configuration of the workforce; coping with discretionary time; skills to engage in meaningful activity; and the accumulation of leisure capital.

With the growing awareness of the inter-connectedness of mind, body, and feeling (Gardner, 1983; Eisner 1985; Reimer, 2000), the func-tionalist knowledge model is becoming less relevant. As such knowledge is considered inadequate, people elect to operate more effectively in a world of accelerating change, knowledge and skills. The acquisition of such skills is to improve the quality of life and to foster personal develop-ment during the lifespan.

Holding a steady job throughout one's working career is fast be-coming a thing of the past (OECD, 1994). Facts, analyses, and strategies of job study undertaken by the OECD (1994) indicate that future workers can expect six or more changes in a working life. The configuration of the workforce into core, flexible contractual fringe, and flexible labor forces (Handy, 1989) have leisure time implications for each of the workforce types. Consequently, coping with discretionary time in self-fulfilling ways will require individuals to engage in meaningful and enriching ac-tivities (Chapman and Aspin, 1997). In a telling message about meaning-ful skill acquisition and activity learning, Kodaly suggested:

> If you really want to lift people from their misery, give them something permanent for themselves, which can never be taken away from them, and which can bolster them in their time of trouble and lift them in their time of joy (cited in Bacon 1969, p. 55).

Although Kodaly was referring to music education, the above message could apply to other leisure and human development pursuits. The exhilaration that accrues from participation in creative activities brings with it intrinsic satisfactions that are the essence of quality lei-sure experiences.

Like the build-up of coral reefs over time, lifelong learning during discretionary time accounts for the accumulation of leisure capital, a con-cept arising from the work of Bourdieu (1985), who focused upon tastes and preferences in art. Leisure capital has general application to all forms of cultural activity and consumption, such as sports, holidays, outdoor recreation, media, home decors, cars, clothes, and drinks. Leisure capital can take forms of economic, cultural, and symbolic goods and resources. Using occupation as the main indicator, Bourdieu studied influences of social class upon leisure activity.

Seniors and those in mid-life build up stocks of leisure capital that could be economic, social, cultural, or physical assets. Economic capital could be savings, investments, and funds for survival and discretionary expenditures. Social and cultural capital are comprised of social relationships, qualifications, attitudes and values, memberships in clubs and associations, activity skills, and informal activities, such as media consumption and home-based leisure. In addition, individuals might have assets such as golf clubs, bicycles, bats, racquets, and reading materials.

Research by the Australian Bureau of Statistics (1998) (ABS) shows that leisure time is distributed in large amounts across the life span. As the following table shows, people over the age of 65 enjoy the largest amount of free time with 429 minutes per day.

Minutes per day (social/community and leisure)			
Age groups	**Men**	**Women**	**Total**
15-24	379	319	350
25-34	282	250	265
34-44	270	253	261
45-54	293	279	286
55-64	360	352	355
65 and Over	441	420	429
Total	325	301	313

Source: ABS 1998, p. 55

Figure 6.1 Daily Leisure Time by Age and Gender, 1997

The above figure suggests that the reduction of leisure time in earlier years is due to work and family commitments. As family commitments decline, for example, by offspring leaving home, extra free time accrues as persons gets older and are still in the workforce. The implications suggest that over the lifespan there are copious amounts of leisure time available for preparation of life during and after paid employment. How does one prepare for that? The answer lies in educating oneself for and in leisure. But one may also ask the question – what type of leisure?

What Type of Leisure?

The dimensions of leisure are time, activity, and experience. Quality of life has to do with experience. However, the availability of time to learn about an activity is essential. Much of leisure may be broadly categorized as casual or serious. Casual leisure is immediately intrinsically reward-ing, relatively short-lived pleasurable activity requiring little or no special training (Stebbins, 1997). Serious leisure is the systematic pursuit of an amateur, hobbyist, or volunteer activity that participants find so sub-stantial, interesting, and fulfilling that, in the typical case, they launch themselves on a career centred on acquiring and expressing its special skills, knowledge, and experience (Stebbins, 1992). Veal and Lynch (2001) depict leisure as having separate fields of the arts and entertain-ment, sports, tourism, play, recreation, hobbies/interests, games, and do-ing nothing. They go on to state that different forms of human activity or inactivity often overlap. Thus, sports are forms of play and sport may also be entertainment. The activities in the separate field may be pursued as casual leisure with little or no learning required. Consequently, the categories of Stebbins (1992) of amateur, hobby, and volunteer activity lend themselves more suitably for lifelong learning. Details of time spent on specific leisure activities by Australians reveal that television watching is the highest on the time scale. There are also gender differences, with men spending more time engaging in sports and watching television and women more time talking and reading (ABS, 1998). The activity profile indicates that time spent in casual leisure is overwhelming and that the proportion of leisure learners motivated by intrinsic satisfaction is com-paratively small.

The quality of life, therefore, that accrues from lifelong learning has much to do with serious rather than casual leisure. However, whereas serious leisure focuses on specific activities, lifelong learning is life-wide and may focus on a variety of activities, many at the same time, through the lifespan. If at the cessation of paid employment, individuals have ac-cumulated leisure capital that they can draw on, then relying on previous learning and preparation, good quality of life is assured. Since this chap-

ter focuses on individuals in mid and later life, some theoretical considerations of aging are appropriate.

Aging Theory and Lifelong Learning

Three major theories have dominated the study of aging – disengagement, activity, and continuity. The disengagement theory first proposed
by Cumming and Henry (1961) viewed aging as separation of and
changes in existing social ties, a general constriction of life space, and an
increasing predisposition with self. It was further proposed that discon-
nection from society could be mutually satisfying for the individual and
society. The lifelong learning philosophy would reject this notion, as the
defining thesis is purposeful learning on an ongoing basis with the aim
of improving knowledge, skills, and competence (Häggström, 2002).
Although older people reduce engagement in physically demanding activities (Gordon and Gaitz, 1976; McGuire and Dottavio, 1986), there is
evidence that they engage in informal social activity that is positively related to life satisfaction (Lemon, Bengston, and Peterson, 1972; Longino
and Kart, 1982). In mid-life Dodd (2004) found individuals who were
unable to participate in physical activities had to substitute with other less
physical or cultural activities. They did not disengage. The problems of
mid-life adaptation are discussed later in this chapter.

Therefore, lifelong learning supports the activity theory which
states that successful aging depends on a person's ability to maintain
social activity and not to disassociate from it. The continuity theory
strengthens the lifelong learning philosophy that successful aging depends on people's competence in adapting to change, an ability that has
developed in their lives (Atchley, 1991). The continuity theory seeks to
identify a variety of patterns of aging, not just a single one. The pathway
to variety is through lifelong learning.

The Development of Age Classes

Longevity of human life has been one of a series of social transformations that have created a new-age class system. As a consequence of industrialization, worldwide changes have occurred for the old, and modern
societies have become rigidly age-stratified. According to Young and
Schuller (1991), the separation of ages has resulted in an age-locked society. Before industrialization economic production by the family yielded a

basic living. Men, women, and children had to work from cradle to grave to subsist. Every consumer had to be producer. People of any age had to work to the limits of their capacities as long as they could. For the elderly this meant working until they dropped (Minois, 1989).

The advent of the factory put an end to the family (men, women, and children) as the unit of production. The factory brought into existence age-classes, which did not exist before. Gains in agricultural and other goods production allowed masses of people for the first time in human history to live above subsistence level (Young and Schuller, 1991). As a consequence, children and older people were gradually removed as bread-winners. Workers had more dependents whose needs were to be satisfied. The removal of the young and the old from the labor force caused a concentration of leisure among children and the aged.

The classes were further regulated by decree of the state. It laid down at what year children should enter school and on what birthdate workers should terminate paid work. In Britain, the state turned men into old men. The variability of leaving ages in recent years has blurred boundaries between the continuation of work and retirement. Young and Schuller (1991) state that the blurring of boundaries is not limited to age, as older people are as trendy in fashion as young persons, and romance is as much for them as for their grandchildren. In the latter half of the twentieth century a number of scholars have turned their attention to the study of aging. Theories have been proposed and debated, but where do they stand with the lifelong learning philosophy?

Age-classes

The Industrial Revolution created three age classes – the young, the workers, and the old. The three age classes could by ranked in terms of status attached to them. The people of working age have the highest status, the young are next as they represent the future, and the old coming last (Young and Schuller, 1991). The boundaries of age-classes have been blurred as young people spend more time in education before they can enter the workforce. Work-ending at the other end of the spectrum has become increasingly variable with some retiring early, others on time, and with the dispensing of the retirement age that is now introduced in some countries, a few decide to carry on well beyond customary retirement age. Therefore, chronological age is no longer a good divider of age classes.

So this chapter refers to the term "third age" as a replacement for retirement. According to Young and Schuller (1991) it is a phase that can now encompass twenty, thirty, or even forty years of active life after leaving work. The origin of the term is French as used in l' Université du Troisième Age – The University of the Third Age. The "term not already tarnished" (Laslett, p. 3) allows aging to be a continuous process, rather than breaking it into stages, with the later years tainted with decline and loss of powers. Thus, Laslett (1989) described the life-course progression: First comes the era of dependence, socialization, immaturity, and education; second an era of independence, maturity, and responsibility, or earning and saving; and third an era of personal fulfilment (p. 4).

Rather than seeing the third age as a period of decline, it is now seen as a phase of opportunity. As more and more people ward off diseases associated with old age, more and more people should be able to lead healthier lives well into later life. For those people in mid-life where work is dominant over leisure, free time for discretionary activity is a lot less than for those in the third age. However, it is an important stage of the life cycle when physical changes to the human self cause problems of activity selection and substitution in leisure. It is a time when lifelong learning offers avenues of personal development.

Era of Independence, Maturity, and Responsibility

Life span development psychologists usually establish the beginning of middle-age as around 40 years of age and continuing to approximately 60-65 years of age (Van-Hoose and Worth, 1982; Gething and Hatchard, 1989; Lefrancois, 1990; Schuster and Ashburn, 1992; Zal, 1992; Papalia and Wendkos Olds, 1995). It is well-documented that during middle adulthood, individuals engage in a process of reassessing traditionally held values associated with family, work, and self (Chiriboga, 1984; Levinson, Darrow, Klein, Levinson, and McKee, 1978; Levinson, 1996; Lowenthal, Thurnher, Chiriboga, 1976). However, there is a paucity of literature on mid-life leisure, with a few studies undertaken in North America (Freysinger, 1987, 1995; Horna, 1987; and Carpenter, 1992, 1993, 1994, 1997). More recently, a study of leisure participation to alleviate problems encountered at mid-life was undertaken by Dodd (2004).

A review of the literature on men by Dodd (2004) illustrated the physical changes that take place at mid-life. Several points emerged:

physical changes are more pronounced than any time since childhood and adolescence; understanding physical changes is essential in understanding how men may adjust to mid-life; appearance and physical condition may set limits on the kinds of work and leisure activities men may pursue at mid-life; those who define themselves in terms of physical fitness or youthful appearance may find the changes hard to accept; physical changes do not affect daily activities, but mid-life is a time when life-threatening diseases emerge; death rates are higher for men than women, with cancer and heart disease the major causes of death. Smoking, diets high in fat, and physical inactivity are major contributing factors; major factors relating to cardiovascular disease include stress, obesity, excessive alcohol consumption, and diabetes. Public agencies concerned with healthy lifestyles focus on smoking and the benefits of low fat diets, but physical activity as a way of life receives less attention. Thirty percent of adult men do not engage in sufficient physical activity to maintain or improve their health, even though moderate physical exercise is known to reduce cardiovascular disease and provide substantial health benefits. The greatest improvement in public health will arise from the sedentary becoming moderately active. Some loss of cognitive abilities takes place at mid-life; by mid-life individuals are believed to think dialectically, which enables them to be more sensitive and tolerant of contradictions; and dialectical thinking is partly responsible for development of creativity that often manifests itself at mid-life.

Dodd's (2004) study revealed that men who preferred physical activities in younger adulthood and could no longer participate in these activities at mid-life found adjustment to leisure participation more difficult, while those who preferred cultural activities were less affected by the decrease in abilities. Participation in physical and cultural activities are not reliant on each other. Hence, a reduced level of involvement in a physically active pastime or even the cessation of an activity was likely to pose fewer difficulties. Dodd's research strengthens the case for life-wide learning in early adulthood, so that as individuals find participation in one activity difficult, they can substitute with another activity or a variety of activities of an appropriate nature and suitable to their middle-aged status. Further, the fact that the development of creativity and dialectic thinking manifests itself in mid-life means that mid-life is a fertile period to learn new activities and even to continue learned activities well into late adulthood. Young people who develop skills with musical instruments can continue these activities well into a later age. Those who have enjoyed football may adapt by participating in a less vigorous activity like golf. However, adjustment to golf is eased if the skills are learned during adolescence and early adulthood.

The Era for Self-fulfillment

The era of personal fulfilment sounds ideal, but in reality there are many people who are miserable and unfulfilled. Thus, the third age as an era of self-fulfilment becomes a potentiality rather than an actuality. But the third age, used in a positive sense, bestows on individuals a certain kind of freedom – "freedom to" rather than "freedom from." The chores of the journey to work, coping with a stressful work environment, and returning during the rush hour are replaced by options of going fishing, playing golf, reading, mowing the lawn, and anything else one wants to do, when and how one wants to do it.

However, not all persons in the third age want such freedom. Indeed, there are many who want to be constrained by the rigors and routine of work and feel comfortable with it; but the argument of this chapter is that those who have a chance will venture out and seek a positive freedom. Berlin (1969) uses the word "liberty" in a positive sense:

> The "positive" sense of the word "liberty" derives from the wish on the part of an individual to be his own master. I wish my life and decisions to depend on myself, not on external forces of whatever kind. I wish to be an instrument of my own, not of other men's, acts of will. I wish to be a subject not an object; to be moved by reasons, by conscious purposes, which are my own, not by causes which affect me, as it were, from outside. I wish to be somebody, not nobody; a doer—deciding, not being decided for, self-decided and not acted upon by external nature or by other men as if I were a thing, or an animal, or a slave incapable of playing the human role, that is, conceiving goals and policies of my own and realising them (p. 131).

The positive form of the third age is the desire to be one's own master, free from the interference of others. However, taking advantage of the opportunity is dependent on many considerations. Money is foremost. Notwithstanding that the time structure on one's existence in between fixed points of meal times and sleep, there are many empty holes in which one has opportunities to make choices – time to play, to be creative, to keep fit, to volunteer services.

On the negative side, there are those who are involuntarily terminated from work. A recent study (Lobo and Parker, 1999) has shown how unemployment can be devastating when people are materially and psychologically deprived. The free time enforced on late career unemployment can diminish one's freedom rather than enlarge it. Their sense of time collapses, and apathy takes over. Thus, the meaning of positive freedom in contemporary society takes on a negative version for many adversely affected by unemployment. It must be said that a small minority are minimally affected, and a smaller proportion actually love their newfound freedom from the stresses of the work environment.

Young and Schuller (1991), in their sample of people in their fifties and early sixties, found that some people were unable to create a new time-structure for themselves when they were no longer in paid work. They were people who had a hard life that got harder when they retired. The work that structured them incapacitated them from taking advantage of their new freedom, demonstrating that the third age needs preparation in the second and the first. Others were able to use their freedom to good effect. They had more variety in their lives than they had while working. The efforts of paid work were substituted by the efforts of unpaid work. Many belonged to the "informal economy" of helping others and doing voluntary work that was chosen by them, and what they wanted to do. Few people had the range of choice these third agers had. It was their freedom with new opportunities.

Aging Well

What is aging well? Several writers (Baltes and Baltes, 1990; Fry et al., 1997) have associated aging well with: (a) good physical functioning and health, such as the absence of disease and disability in combination with sustained functional independence; (b) positive mental health, perceived happiness and life satisfaction, as well as functional independence to maintain daily activities; (c) material security, such as having adequate shelter, sustenance, and economic resources; and (d) sustained sociability with social support, social networks, social competence, and meaningful daily activities. The contribution of leisure learning to daily activities, life satisfaction, and functional independence does much for self-fulfillment and social development. It was Voltaire who said, "the one who has not the spirit of his age has all the unhappiness" (Letter to Madame du Châtelet).

A current term used for successful aging is one coined by John McLeish (1976). He used the words "Ulyssean adult" to describe those individuals who continue to seek new adventures and opportunities in their later years; not unlike Homer's Ulysses, who after 50 years of life sought adventures, and who at age 70 embarked on his last journey. The freedom to embark on any journey of personal growth is now in the grasp of the middle and third agers. Whereas losses may be experienced due to the aging process, strategies of compensation may be used to continue the lifestyle of one's choosing. Baltes and Baltes (1990) have suggested three interacting elements: (a) selection—which refers to restricting one's world to fewer domains or activities in order to focus on those areas that are a high priority; (b) optimization—or engaging in behaviors selected to maximize functioning through practice and technology, thereby allowing pursuit of desired activities and; (c) compensation—which revolves around using adaptive techniques such as using higher wattage lighting for reading, designed to compensate for losses of functioning or floatation devices to assist with better swimming. The quality of life can be enhanced through leisure by involving oneself in a variety of learning pathways as the following section illustrates.

Enhancement of Quality of Life

McGuire and Tedrick (2000) have suggested approaches that will help aging individuals to use leisure as a tool for personal development and further learning. They include programming for growth, use of technology, active learning, creativity, physically and mentally challenging activities, volunteerism, intergenerational activities, social activities, and spiritual activities.

Leisure providers should recognize the potential for growth in middle and later life. Growth comes from challenge, and challenge comes from freedom to experiment. Dated, age-related attitudes should be replaced by those that recognize opportunities and encourage experimentation.

The enthusiastic adoption of the use of new technologies and the eagerness to share these skills with others is a positive way of staying current and absorbing knowledge. The use of e-mail, the internet, and e-commerce allows many to stay informed and keep abreast of the latest equipment and products.

Involvement in active learning is growing worldwide with an array of opportunities in which aging adults may participate. Community education offerings in the field of leisure are varied and are promoted through multi-media modes.

Creativity is an essential element in challenging and self-fulfilling aging. Creativity comes in various forms. Middle-aged and older adults are capable of ingenious approaches to life's challenges.

Physically and mentally challenging activities are known to maintain and improve the domains of biological, cognitive, and psychological functioning. There is much evidence that today's seniors are more vibrant than chronological age might suggest.

Volunteerism and intergenerational activities are a wonderful way in which seniors influence and are influenced by younger generations. The passing on of skills and knowledge through voluntary engagement does much to enhance Delors' "working together pillar." Grandchildren teaching grandparents how to use the Internet is an example of younger generations influencing older people by way of learning.

Meaningful social contact has also been shown to contribute to life satisfaction. Programs that include social components, such as community dancing, sing-alongs, and group games, result in an accumulation of pleasurable social benefits. These gains add to the life satisfaction.

Purists would see spirituality as the essence of leisure. Through religious and spiritual activities, opportunities to learn abound. As people grow older, their age is a fertile ground for leisure involvement.

Recent research supports these approaches to enhancing quality of life as one gets older. Consequently, the middle and third ages may be looked upon as life phases of creativity, experimentation, freedom, and opportunity. It is therefore possible to prepare through the lifecycle for a third age that is self-fulfilling, and to develop socially through lifelong learning using this highly desirable vehicle we call leisure.

Conclusion

The life-course was viewed as a continuous process imperceptibly linking the phases of dependence, immaturity, and education to independence, maturity, responsibility, and further, to the era of self-fulfilment. Viewing life as a continuous process, leisure education should have its beginnings in childhood and adolescence as described in the preceding chapter. This chapter focused on the importance of leisure education and lifelong learning in enhancing the quality of life in middle and late years of the lifecycle. The vehicle for this advancement is serious leisure. The chapter has shown that individuals have copious amounts of leisure time throughout the lifecycle. Those in the third age have greater amounts of free time when compared to their mid-life cohorts and can still choose from a variety of activities, particularly if they have recourse to the lifelong learning strategy. At their time of life, the ability to be creative and think dialectically will aid in making appropriate decisions. For the third agers, the concepts of freedom and opportunity were presented as conditions for making appropriate choices to enhance the quality of life.

References

Atchley, R. C. (1991). *Social forces in later life* (6th ed.). Belmont, CA: Wadsworth.

Australian Bureau of Statistics. (1998). *How Australians use their time* (Cat. No. 4152.0) ABS, Canberra.

Bacon, D. (1969). Kodaly and Orf – Report from Europe. *Music Educators Journal, 55*(8), 53–56.

Baltes, P. B. and Baltes, M. M. (1990). *Successful aging: Perspectives from the behavioural sciences*. New York: Cambridge University Press.

Berlin, I. (1969). *Four essays on liberty*. London: Oxford University Press.

Bourdieu, P. (1985). *Distinction: A social critique of the judgement of taste*. London: Routledge & Kegan Paul.

Carpenter, G. (1992). Adult perceptions of leisure: life experiences and life structure. *Society and Leisure, 15*(2), 587–606.

Carpenter, G. (1993). Leisure and health during middle adulthood: a case study. In D. M. Compton and S. E. Iso-Ahola (Eds.), *Leisure and mental health*. Park City, UT: Family Development Resources, pp. 98–111.

Carpenter, G. (1994) *A study of leisure during adulthood*. Miscellaneous paper. University of Oregon.

Carpenter, G. (1997). A longitudinal investigation of mid-life men who hold leisure in higher regard than work. *Society and Leisure, 20*(1), pp. 189–211.

Chapman, J. and Aspin, D. (1997). *The school, the community and life-long learning*. London: Cassell.

Chiriboga, D. A. (1984). The longitudinal study of transitions. In Mednick, S. A., Harway, M., and Finello, K. M. (Eds.) *Handbook of longitudinal research volume two* (pp. 340–355). New York: Praeger.

Cumming E. and Henry, W. E. (1961). *Growing old: The process of disengagement*. New York: Basic Books.

Delors, J. (1996). *Learning: The treasure within*. International Commission on Education for the Twenty-First Century. Paris: Unesco.

Dodd, J. (2004). The capacity of leisure participation to alleviate problems encountered at mid-life. In F. H. Fu, D. Markus, and T. K. Tong (Eds.), *Negative events in the lifecycle: Leisure and recreation as a counteraction* (pp. 58–81). Hong Kong, China: Professional Publications Co.

Du Bois-Reymond, M. (1999). Trend-setters and other types of lifelong learners. In P. Alheit, J. Beck, E. Kammler, R. Taylor, and H. S. Olesen (Eds.), *Lifelong learning inside and outside schools: Collected papers of the European conference on lifelong learning* (2nd ed., pp. 360–375). Roskilde, Denmark: Roskilde University Press. Abstract retrieved February 16, 2004, from http://www.erill.uni-bremen.de/lios/sections/s4_bois.html.

Eisner, E. (Ed.). (1985). *Learning and teaching the ways of knowing*. Chicago: University of Chicago Press.

Freysinger, V. (1987). The meaning of leisure in middle adulthood. *Journal of Physical Education, Recreation and Dance, 58*(8), pp. 40–45.

Freysinger, V. (1995). The dialectics of leisure and development for women and men in mid-life: An interpretive study. *Journal of Leisure Research, 27*(1), pp. 61–84.

Fry, C. L., Dickerson-Putman, J., Draper, P., Ikels, C. Keith, J., Glascock, A. P., and Harpending, H.C. (1997). Culture and meaning of a good old age. In J. Sokolovsky (Ed.), *The culture context of aging—Worldwide perspectives* (2nd ed.) (pp. 99–123). Westport, CT: Bergin & Garvey.

Gardner, H. (1983). *Frames of mind: The theory of multiple intelligences*. New York: Basic Books.

Gething, L. and Hatchard, D. (Eds.). (1989). *Life span development*. Sydney: McGraw-Hill.

Gordon, C. and Gaitz, C. (1976). Leisure and lives: Expressivity across the life span. In R. Bintock and E. Shanas (Eds.), *Handbook of aging and the social sciences*. New York: Van Nostrand Reinhold.

Häggström, B. M., (2002). *Sources of knowledge, spaces for learning*. Retrieved February 6, 2004, from http://www.eblida.org/topics/lifelong/ifla_paper.htm

Handy, C. (1989). *The age of unreason*. London: Arrow.

Haw, G. and Hughes, P. (Eds.), (1998). *Education for the twenty-first century in the Asia-Pacific region*. Report on the Melbourne UNESCO Conference, Australian Commission of UNESCO, Victoria.

Horna, J. (1987). The process of choosing leisure activities and preferences: A stream model. *Society and Leisure, 10*(2), pp. 219–234.

Laslett, P. A. (1989). *A fresh map of life*. London: Weidenfeld and Nicolson.

Lefrancois, G. R. (1990). *The lifespan,* (3rd ed). Belmont, CA: Wadsworth Publishing Co.

Lemon, B. W., Bengston, V. L., and Peterson, J. A. (1972). An exploration of the activity theory of aging: Activity types and life satisfaction among inmovers to a retirement community. *Journal of Gerontology, 27,* 511–523.

Levinson, D. J. (1996). *The seasons of a woman's life.* New York: Alfred A. Knopf.

Levinson, D. J., Darrow, C. N., Klein, E. B., Levinson, M. H., and McKee, B. (1978). *The seasons of a man's life.* New York: Alfred A. Knopf.

Lowenthal, M. F., Thurnher, M., and Chiriboga, D. A. (1976). *Four stages of life.* San Francisco: Jossey-Bass.

Lobo, F. and Parker, S. (1999). *Late career unemployment: Impacts on self, family and lifestyle.* Melbourne: Hepper Marriott.

Longino, C. F. and Kart, C. S. (1982). Explicating activity theory: A formal replication. *Journal of Gerontology, 37,* 713–722.

Longworth, N. (Ed.) (1995). An action agenda for lifelong learning for the 21st century. Part one of the report from the First Global Conference on Lifelong Learning. Rome, Italy, 30 November–2 December 1994. Brussels: World Initiative on Lifelong Learning.

Minois, J. (1989). *History of old age: From antiquity to the renaissance.* Cambridge, UK: Polity Press.

McGuire, F. A. and Dottavio, F. D. (1986). Outdoor recreation participation across the lifespan: Abandonment, continuity or liberation? *International Journal of Aging and Human Development, 24,* 87–100.

McGuire, F. and Tedrick, R. (2000). Ulssyean aging: Human development and leisure. In M. Cabeza (Ed.), *Leisure and human development: 6th World Leisure Congress Proposals.* Bilbao, Spain: University of Deusto, pp. 153–158.

McLeish, J. (1976). *The Ulyssean adult: Creativity in middle and later years.* Toronto: McGraw-Hill Ryerson.

Nazareth, T. (1999). *Lifelong learning: Music education for adult beginners.* Unpublished PhD thesis, University of Western Australia.

OECD (1994). *Jobs study—Facts, analysis, strategies.* Paris: OECD.

OECD (1996). *Making lifelong learning a reality for all.* Paris: OECD.

Papalia, D. E. and Wendkos Olds, S. (1995). *Human development.* New York: McGraw-Hill.

Reimer, B. (2000). Why do humans value music? In C. K. Madsen (Ed.), *Vision 2020: The Housewright symposium on the future of music education* (pp. 25–54). USA: MENC.

Schuster, C. S. and Ashburn, S. S. (Eds.), (1992). *The process of human development: A holistic life-span approach*. Philadelphia: J.B. Lippincott Co.

Stebbins, R. A. (1997). Casual leisure: A conceptual statement. *Leisure Studies, 16,* 17–25.

Stebbins, R. A. (1992). *Amateurs, professionals, and serious leisure.* Montreal, QC and Kingston, ON: McGill-Queen's University Press.

Van-Hoose, W. H. and Worth, M. R. (1982). *Adulthood in the life cycle.* Dubuque, IA: Wm. C. Brown.

Veal, T. and Lynch, R. (2001). *Australian leisure* (2nd ed). Sydney: Longman.

Young, M. and Schuller, T. (1991). *Life after work: The arrival of the ageless society.* London: Harper Collins.

Zal, H. M. (1992). *The sandwich generation: Caught between growing children and aging parents.* New York: Insight Books.

Chapter Seven
Leisure Education for Special Groups
by Ian Patterson

Introduction

Historically, people with special needs such as those with disabilities, those who are unemployed, and those who are retired have been looked down upon and treated poorly by society. This is because our culture devalues people who are not working, and as a result, they are less likely to have valued social roles (McGill, 1996). Many of these marginal groups are reliant on government support resulting in a lifetime of dependency, because many are unlikely to work in open employment. The economic rationalist would argue that they are a continual drain on society's resources and as such should be regarded as noncontributing citizens.

As a result, people with special needs spend an inordinate amount of time concentrating on their survival needs, such as where they will live and what sort of care and support is available in the community, and they have an enormous amount of free time at their disposal. Even though they have large amounts of free time at their disposal, leisure services have rarely been seen as a priority for these groups of people. Our Western society values paid work. The Protestant Work Ethic became popular after the Industrial Revolution and was based on Puritan ideals that advocated the importance of "honest toil" and working hard. Religious leaders supported the 14-hour day as part of the wholesome discipline of factory life, and expressed strong antagonism against play, enjoyment, and pleasure. At the same time, they emphasized the importance of "The ethic of serving God by extreme restraint, by giving up pleasure, by constant work and the accumulation of the means for spreading the material basis for work" (De Grazia, 1964, p. 27).

Since the Industrial Revolution, work has provided stability and structure to people's lives. It offers a sense of personal identification and creative satisfaction. Paid employment also provides a means for economic independence, and has been regarded as central to the development of self-concept, peer relationships, and basic identity in life (Kraus, 2001). As Moos (1989, p. 6) explains, "A job can provide structure for a person's life, a sense of satisfaction and productivity that stems from completing meaningful tasks, a feeling of belonging to a valued reference group, a basis for self-esteem and personal identity."

On the other hand, leisure was not seen as a basic survival need and as a result was frequently trivialized as unimportant (McNeil and Anderson, 1999). Yet leisure has been found to be an essential ingredient of people's lives, making time more bearable, helping to relieve stress and tensions, to build and maintain relationships, and to relieve boredom (McGill, 1996). McGill (1996) summarized the benefits of leisure as, "Through our leisure involvements we have gained a stronger sense of who we are, and have strengthened our sense of belonging" (p. 7). With this in mind, Kraus (1994) has challenged us to promote leisure with his plea to endorse leisure education to all groups in society and to not just target children in the school system:

> What is needed are programs of leisure education which promote forms of play that are physically and emotionally enriching, that are inexpensive and readily available, and that contribute to healthy lives and positive human relationships. While in the past leisure education was directed chiefly at schoolchildren, today it is needed by all age groups and must be provided in many different kinds of community settings. (p. 45)

This chapter will discuss the importance of leisure education to the lives of people who have special needs. It proposes that governments and service delivery agencies need to place greater emphasis on leisure education programs that support the development of "serious" leisure skills and abilities (see Chapter 1) and not merely to provide diversional or time filling activities on a casual basis. A leisure education program provides the skills, confidence, and abilities to develop competency levels for the future development of serious lifetime pursuits. For many people with special needs, open employment may no longer be a serious option, and because of this, they are destined to a life of meaningless, empty, and boring free time. Alternatively, serious leisure can provide the social role competencies and benefits that are similar to those that are achieved through open employment. Therefore, the aim of this chapter is to explore the current literature to ascertain whether people with special needs who undertake a leisure education program will successfully develop the skills and competencies of serious leisure activities, and as a result, contribute to their quality of life.

Leisure Boredom

Leisure boredom has been regarded as one of the major problems in our society. As far back as in the 1960s, Brightbill (1961) wrote that boredom is something that none of us can avoid, and for some of us it can have devastating effects: "Some of the young go haywire, run in gangs as hoodlums, kill themselves playing chicken in hot rods, and in the cities get 'hooked' by dope pushers" (p. 62).

Most of the recent studies on leisure boredom have been conducted on adolescents and youth because they are regarded as becoming more easily bored than other age groups (Caldwell, Smith, and Weissinger, 1992; Shaw, Caldwell, and Kleiber, 1996; Patterson, Pegg, and Dobson-Patterson, 2000).) Boredom has been conceptualized as a state of under-stimulation, under-arousal, lack of momentum, or a lack of psychological involvement associated with dissatisfaction in the task situation (Brissett and Snow, 1993; Larson and Richards, 1991). On the other hand, leisure boredom has been explained by Iso-Ahola and Weissinger (1990) as, "The subjective perception that available leisure experiences are not sufficient to instrumentally satisfy needs for optimal arousal... [leisure activities] are not sufficiently frequent, involving, exciting, varied, or novel" (p. 5).

Several researchers have suggested that occupying one's time by generating and engaging in interesting leisure activities may result in the reduction of boredom. Iso-Ahola and Weissinger (1990) concluded that individuals who possess a varied assortment of leisure skills would be unlikely to encounter boredom as a problem during their leisure time. Alternatively, those who reject adult structures are more likely to engage in self-defeating health behaviors such as cigarette smoking, juvenile delinquency, and alcohol and drug abuse (Caldwell and Smith, 1995; Wegner, Flisher, Muller, and Lombard, 2006).

Furthermore, it has been suggested that filling one's time with activities is beneficial in offsetting the negative psychological effects (such as boredom) related to unemployment (Jahoda, 1982; Warr, 1987). Hepworth (1980) found that unemployed workers' ability to structure their time was the best predictor of their mental health.

Individuals who are able to occupy their time creatively are less likely to experience depression and anxiety, both of which have been shown to be significantly related to boredom (Vodanovich, Verner, and Gilbride, 1991).

Therefore the research suggests that the leisure boredom effect occurs when leisure is not always perceived as positive. That is, "free time" is seen as something that individuals cannot escape from, or as a means of encouraging a meaningless leisure routine. This may also refer to individuals who are constrained from participating in satisfying leisure activities, lack the motivation, or when leisure pursuits are enforced on those who do not have sufficient leisure competence. Leisure education has been suggested as an important area to counter the effects of leisure boredom.

Leisure Education

The term "leisure education" is mainly referred to as a process rather than as mere content. Mundy (1998) described it as "…a total developmental process through which individuals develop an understanding of leisure, of the self in relation to leisure, and of the relationship among leisure, their own lifestyle, and society" (p. 5).

Mundy (1998) focuses on the process rather than the content of leisure education and described it as a total developmental process, to help determine where leisure fits into individuals' lives, and if it is compatible with their values, needs, and goals. Mundy categorized leisure education into four main components:

    1. Leisure Awareness
- This involves broadening knowledge about leisure, what it is, and why it should be an essential part of one's life. That is…
- What is leisure?
- What are the benefits and outcomes of leisure experiences?
- Taking personal responsibility for a leisure lifestyle.

    Behavioral Outcomes
- Understanding the concept of leisure and applying it to one's life.
- Acknowledging and accepting personal responsibility for one's own leisure.
- Identifying a variety of potential leisure experiences.

    2. Self-Awareness
- Understanding personal attitudes and perspectives about leisure.
- Examining oneself in relation to important social networks.
- Identifying personal motives and social factors related to participation.

- Recognizing the appropriateness of personal and social behaviors.

Behavioral Outcomes

- Understanding how one's interests, values, attitudes and needs interact with and impact leisure experiences.

3. Leisure Skills
   - This component is about acquiring leisure skills so that they become a meaningful part of one's lifestyle. People cannot enjoy participating in leisure activities if they do not feel competent.
   - It involves teaching specific skills requiring the use of instructional strategies and techniques.
   - It ensures that appropriate activities and skills are acquired through leisure counseling.

   Behavioral Outcomes
   - Utilizes decision making, problem solving, planning and evaluation processes to achieve leisure goals.
   - Possesses social interaction skills needed for leisure satisfaction.

4. Leisure Resources
   - Uses leisure resources for enhancing and enriching leisure experiences. This looks at what is available, where, and for how much money. For example, special discounts on transportation and admission prices are available in the community through public and private leisure services.

   Behavioral Outcomes
   - Identifies and utilizes personal, community, and environmental resources for leisure experiences.
   - Evaluates and utilizes leisure products, equipment, and places for their worth and usefulness and their contribution to leisure goals.

Leisure education has been promoted as a modality that not only increases people's awareness about the importance of leisure but also encourages a sense of personal control and competence (Datillo and Murphy, 1991). In fact, many leisure scholars have suggested that the promotion of independent living should be the ultimate goal of leisure education programs for people with special needs (Bullock and Howe, 1991; Bullock and Luken, 1994). The challenge for educators and leisure professionals is to help people of every age appreciate the important contribution of leisure to the personal health and well-being and community life, and to introduce and strengthen positive human values that influence recreation and play (Kraus, 1994).

In September of 1998, the World Leisure and Recreation Association approved an International Position Statement on leisure education and populations with special needs (World Leisure and Recreation Association, 2001). In its preamble, it acknowledged the fact that:

> A community's vision should be inclusive of all its individuals, embodying a clear value of commitment to enhance access to leisure opportunities for individuals with special needs. Therefore it should be recognized that leisure education programs for people with special needs play important roles in improving the quality of community life.

In this statement, the association distinguished between two forms of leisure: serious and casual (see Chapter 1).

Leisure Education and People with Disabilities

The basic human rights of people with special needs have been slow to be recognized, and it was not until the later half of the 20th century that humane legislation and policy changes began to be put into place, especially for people with disabilities (the Australian Disability Discrimination Act of 1992; the Americans with Disabilities Act of 1990; the UK Disability Discrimination Act of 1995, and the Human Rights Act of 1998). The provision of leisure services has been even slower to respond to these legislative changes in government policy because of the unfounded belief that people with special needs lacked the necessary abilities and competencies to warrant the provision of long-term leisure activity programs.

However, this slowly changed as leisure professionals and educators began to institute leisure education programs for people with disabilities. These programs were designed to teach students to access leisure resources in their communities, gain leisure skills, have experience in decision making and self-determination, and increase social skills that were valuable in increasing their social integration (Datillo and St. Peter, 1991). They were first established to prepare adolescents with disabilities to help them enjoy their free time, as well as reduce the need for constant supervision and control by others (Schleien and Ray, 1988). This helped to not only increase their levels of self-determination, but also assisted in community participation and inclusion (Dattilo, 1994).

Leisure education has also been found to be an essential element for people with intellectual disabilities, particularly as they grow older. In addition, research has shown that for people with intellectual disabilities, participation in leisure activities that involves motor skills and social interaction declines during the individual's mid-to-late thirties. For people with Down Syndrome, this decline appears to begin earlier, often during their twenties (Brown, Bayer, and Brown, 1992). As a result, several researchers (Lockwood, Lockwood, and O'Meara, 1991; Bedini, Bullock, and Driscoll, 1993; Neumayer and Bleasdale, 1996; Hoge and Wilhite, 1997) have recommended that increased emphasis needed to be placed on leisure education and counseling programs to actively participate in physically healthy programs, to empower people with intellectual disabilities to make their own decisions, to discover new information and resources about leisure, and to help them in their successful transition from school to adult life.

Lockwood, Lockwood, and O'Meara (1991) supported the importance of developing decision-making skills when experiencing leisure. The authors suggested that there is a need for leisure counseling to encourage a better understanding of the decision making process in nonthreatening and relaxed settings. These might include using such teaching aids as pictures, posters, and audiocassettes to assist people with intellectual disabilities to identify different leisure dimensions and values. Bedini, Bullock, and Driscoll (1993) studied the effects of a leisure education program on 38 high school adolescents with mental retardation so as to help them develop the skills required for transition from school to adult life. The leisure education program involved units on leisure awareness, self-awareness in leisure, leisure opportunities, community resource awareness, barriers, personal resources, planning an outing, outing evaluation, and future plans. Their results found strong positive changes were found in the areas of competence, perceived control, communication social skills, self-esteem, feelings about leisure, life satisfaction, and feelings about life.

Heller, Factor, Sterns, and Sutton (1996) also found that older adults with intellectual disabilities successfully responded to a program centered on leisure education. They used a "person-centered planning for later life curriculum" with a sample of 70 adults who were aged 35 years and older with Down Syndrome, and 50 years and over with mental retardation. The training was conducted in small groups of five to seven people with weekly two-hour classes over 15 sessions. The study found that the greatest improvement was observed in the area of leisure education, and by their last session, trainees were able to understand such concepts as retirement and volunteering. The researchers concluded that one of the main benefits from their study was the increased use of community-based leisure activities for trainees who lived at home.

Hoge, Datillo, and Williams (1999) successfully trialed a leisure education program on two groups of high school students with mild to moderate mental retardation (intervention group n = 19; control group n = 21). The leisure education course consisted of five units taught over 18 weeks for a total of 54 hours of classroom instruction (3 X week, 1 hour sessions). The units were on leisure appreciation, social interaction and friendship, leisure resources, self-determination, and decision making. Leisure coaches were trained to assist participants to engage in community programs, and family and friends were involved by meeting with the leisure coach to discuss the project. The results found that adolescents with mental retardation who participated in the leisure education program had slightly higher scores in perceived freedom in leisure than those who did not participate. Hoge et al. (1999) concluded that, "Leisure education can lead to outcomes important in assisting adolescents with disabilities transition to adult life" (p. 329).

These studies suggest that people with intellectual disabilities benefit from a leisure education program that emphasizes the teaching of motor skills, social skills training, decision making, and how to access new leisure information and resources. With a focus on leisure education, people with disabilities soon learned to develop the skills and competencies that are necessary for participation in leisure experiences. They also became more confident to use community-based resources and to establish new networks of friends that are regarded as the foundation of the social inclusion process.

Leisure Education and Unemployed People

Employment is a dominant force that shapes the patterns of our leisure. This assumption is apparent in noting how difficult it is to apply traditional concepts of leisure to people who are not employed (e.g., Glyptis, 1989; Wearing and Wearing, 1988). The issue of unemployment is of particular importance for women, who historically have faced exclusion or discrimination in the work force. The definition of work as actual employment has hidden and devalued much of the work that women do, and it obscures the relationship between leisure and work (Dattilo, Dattilo, Samdahl, and Kleiber, 1994).

However, there is some evidence to support the fact that there is lower than average participation rates by unemployed individuals and their dependents in organized recreation activities (Simmons, 1988). In a study of 335 Park and Recreation Directors in all States of the USA, Havitz and Spigner (1992) found that unemployed residents were less likely to be granted price concessions than senior citizens, children, low-income residents, and students. Havitz and Spigner (1992) concluded that, "…the unemployed are most at risk for lack of access to recreational services at a time when, for their own health and well-being, they need it most" (p. 43).

Research has shown that as the length of unemployment increases, the number of expensive leisure activities decreases. That is, in-home leisure activities increased (such as watching television), while other types of leisure activities decreased (especially travel, entertainment, and sport). Participation in sports activities was important for unemployed males because of its relatively inexpensive nature and easy accessibility. With gender differences, males tended to participate more in leisure activities than females, as well as more active lifestyles outside the home (Pesavento Raymond, 1992). According to Roberts (1997) the leisure of young people becomes impoverished as a result of unemployment. The range of activities is not reduced, but the frequency of participation decreases because of the lowered income. Lobo (1997/2001) concluded from his studies on unemployed youth in Australia that unemployment excludes people from leisure. That is, they are restricted in their leisure as a result of material and psychological deprivation, and have often been referred to as the new underclass. Their low motivation levels also restrict them from leisure participation, and as a result they need access to leisure education and counseling programs to make them aware of leisure programs that are affordable to them. Therefore, leisure education and counseling seem to be important strategies particularly for unemployed women who spend a great deal of time in the home.

There is a strong argument that states that a sense of worth and value can be obtained from family, leisure, and other social roles (Haworth and Evans, 1987). However, there has been little research about how leisure helps people to cope with the negative effects of unemployment. Pesavento-Raymond (1992) has summarized several of the studies on leisure and unemployment and has suggested that leisure educators should focus more on leisure activities that are fitness and health orientated and low-cost, such as bicycling, walking, and going to the gym.

Other activities such as cooperative and trust games, special events (such as Walk for AIDS), and intergenerational activities (such as day trips and volunteering) help to promote social networking opportunities and can be successful alternatives to boredom, helping to mitigate the negative psychological effects of unemployment. Leisure service providers can do more and offer increased opportunities (such as reduced prices) to develop a sense of competence and self-worth through programs and initiatives that specifically target the unemployed. Stebbins (1992) concluded that serious leisure is an important antidote to, "...the dreary state of unemployment" (p. 133).

Leisure Education and Older Adults

Older adults have more free time than their predecessors because they are spending less time sleeping, eating, and grooming themselves (Robinson and Werner, 1997). In fact, Americans ages 65 and older in 1995 had seven more hours of weekly free time than older people had in 1985. However, more than half of this newly acquired free time is spent on TV viewing. Stebbins (2001) referred to television viewing as a casual leisure activity, one that too steady a diet of can cause "...a sort of psychological dyspepsia, a sense of ennui and listlessness rooted in the unsettling realization that one's life is unfolding in a way largely, if not entirely, devoid of any significant excitement" (p. 54).

As people age, they may become less interested in expanding their leisure repertoire, while others actually cease their participation in some leisure activities (Searle, Mactavish, and Brayley, 1993). This has been found to have important implications for the health and well-being of older adults. Tabourne (1992) suggested that there are three major goals of leisure education for older people who have recently retired from work. Firstly, to help them redefine leisure as not just activities but with a broader perspective. This recognizes the importance of family and friends and past work associates, and the development of new relationships as a leisure experience. Secondly, to enhance older people's self-esteem by fostering leisure independence through effective decision making about leisure. Thirdly, there is a need to supplement health-promoting attitudes and behavior so as to decrease the need for health-care services and drugs.

In addition, the erosion of a sense of personal control and competence is acute among the elderly (Baltes and Baltes, 1990). Institutional care for older adults often undercuts rather than promotes a sense of independent living (Langer and Rodin, 1976; Rodin and Langer, 1977). Because leisure is important to older adults, leisure activities have been used as a tool to enhance older adults' sense of control and competence (Larson, Mannell, and Zuzanek, 1986). Searle and Mahon have attempted to provide research evidence to support the relationship between leisure education programs and the well-being of older adults. In one of their earlier studies, Searle and Mahon (1991) attempted to determine the effects of a leisure education program on the psychological well-being of elderly patients in a day hospital. An experimental group received a leisure education program that occurred one hour per week for eight weeks. A test battery was administered to both groups, before and after the program, to assess the effect of the leisure education program on three dependent variables: locus of control, perceived competence, and self-esteem. The results were statistically significant, indicating that the group who received the leisure education program had a higher sense of perceived leisure competence than the control group. The findings of this study provided tentative support for the proposition that a leisure education program can enhance the well-being of older adults.

In a further study, Mahon and Seale (1994) conducted a further field experiment in a day hospital in Canada. The sample consisted of 22 subjects in the experimental group (mean age 76.8), and 22 in the control group (mean age 77.7). The experimental group was given a leisure education program that occurred for one hour per week for eight weeks. This program was comprised of various written, oral, and audiovisual activities designed to improve factors such as knowledge of leisure resources and leisure-related skills, and/or to assess general lifestyle so as to better understand the role of leisure in an individual's life. Results of this study indicated that the leisure education program had a significant effect on leisure participation and life satisfaction. More specifically, the experimental group displayed significantly higher levels of leisure participation and life satisfaction, compared to the control group at the first post-test.

This study demonstrated that an eight-week leisure education program provided within a day hospital for older adults achieved short-term effects on their leisure participation and life satisfaction. This result provides tentative support for the proposition that leisure education can positively affect the health and well-being of older adults. As a result, leisure education is seen as an effective way to reduce the gap that emerges between environmental demands and an aging person's abilities (Verbrugge, 1990). This gap often results in a process of disablement and dependency. Mahon and Searle (1994) concluded that older adults who can acquire new leisure pursuits strengthen their involvement in existing ones, and who can adapt activities or equipment to sustain their involvement may enjoy longer periods of independence and happier lives.

Searle et al. (1995) further demonstrated the efficacy of leisure education in enhancing personal leisure control and leisure competence as well as the psychological well-being of older adults. Thirteen experimental group subjects (15 controls) went through an extensive leisure education protocol based on Bullock and Howe's (1991) model. Subjects in the experimental group experienced higher levels of perceived leisure control, leisure competence, and life satisfaction, and they reduced their levels of boredom when compared to the control group. The data supports the potential of leisure education as an effective means for promoting a sense of independence among older adults.

In-home leisure education programs have also been found to be important for older people who have had a stroke (Nour, Desrosiers, and Gauthier, 2002). The leisure education program that was used by the experimental group involved 12 steps comprised of 10 intervention sessions, with the final aim to achieve "...leisure satisfaction and the autonomous practice of leisure" (p. 51). The results confirmed that the experimental group was successful and had the desired effects of significantly enhancing total and physical quality of life. However, the researchers obtained nonsignificant results for the level of depression and psychological quality of life. The small sample size of the two

Table 7.1 Means and Standard Deviations for Leisure and Life Satisfaction and Leisure Participation (Mahon and Searle, 1994, p. 39).

| | Dependent Variable | | | | | |
| | PRE-TEST | | POST-TEST | | FOLLOW-UP | |
	Mean	S.D.	Mean	S.D.	Mean	S.D.
Leisure Satisfaction Control	3.43	(.30)	3.49	(.32)	3.47	(.33)
Experimental	3.72	(.49)	3.88	(.47)	3.68	(.48)
Life Satisfaction Control	3.32	(.34)	3.29	(.43)	3.36	(.41)
Experimental	3.25	(.47)	3.40	(.35)*	3.28	(.50)
Leisure Participation Control	1.91	(.21)	1.87	(.12)	1.83	(.18)
Experimental	2.01	(.30)	1.99	(.30)*	1.99	(.26)

Dependent variables were measured on 5-point Likert-type scale. Higher scores reflected higher levels of satisfaction and participation.

* *Significant at the .05 level.*

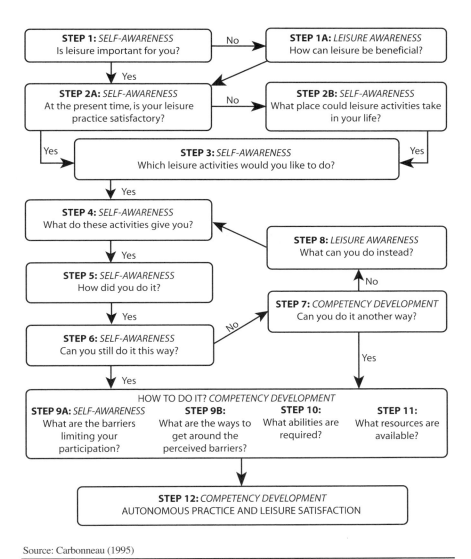

Source: Carbonneau (1995)

FIGURE 7.1 Summary of the Leisure Educational Program

groups of 6 and 7 participants was regarded as a limiting factor for this study.

Therefore, when older adults retire, they have more time than ever before to spend on leisure activities. Many, however, do not know what to do with themselves as they have not planned for their retirement.

Generally, as people age they have reduced, and even ceased participation in some leisure activities, which has negative implications for their health and well-being. Leisure education programs are important for older people to help them redefine leisure as not just activities, but also to help them recognize the importance of family, friends, and past work associates, as well as how to develop new relationships in a leisure context. In institutional care, Searle and Mahon conducted a number of field experiments and found that a leisure education program had significant effects on the experimental group of older people in regard to their leisure participation, leisure control, leisure competence, and life satisfaction. The findings of their studies provided tentative support for the proposition that a leisure education program can enhance the well-being of older adults.

Conclusion

Stebbins (2000) stated that in his view, leisure education should focus more on serious leisure and that sessions need to consist mainly of imparting knowledge about its nature, costs, and rewards, as well as helping people with special needs to participate in specific serious leisure activities. He further suggested that leisure education programs should concentrate on the training of people with special needs to encourage their participation in an amateur, hobbyist, or a career volunteer activity. That is, to inform them in more detail about one or more activities that appeals to them, and how to begin the process of participating in these preferred activities.

Patterson (2000, 2001) has also been a strong advocate of the importance of leisure education programs for people with special needs, and has suggested that they need to focus on developing skills and competencies that are necessary for successful participation in serious leisure experiences. As a result, they will become more confident to use community-based resources, and to establish networks of friends that are the foundation for the social inclusion process. Leisure education can also provide the remedy to help solve the social problem of boredom and meaningless leisure.

This chapter has challenged the belief that leisure experiences are not important for people with special needs, and concludes that it is imperative to develop and fund leisure education programs that focus on the long-term development of leisure skills and competencies. Serious leisure activities (such as amateurism, hobbies, and volunteer work) have been found to be challenging. They also require a great deal of commitment, are valued by the community, and contain a status system and a network of devotees, colleagues, and friends. This forms the basis for self-respect and self-esteem and leads to greater acceptance and inclusion for people with special needs in the community.

References

Baltes, P. B. and Baltes, M. M. (Eds.). (1990). *Successful aging: Perspectives from the behavioral sciences*. Cambridge, UK: Cambridge University Press.

Bedini, L. A., Bullock, C., and Driscoll, L. (1993). The effects of leisure education on factors contributing to the successful transition of students with mental retardation from school to adult life. *Therapeutic Recreation Journal, 27*, 70–82.

Brightbill, C. K. (1961). *Man and leisure: A philosophy of recreation*. Engleworth Cliffs, NJ: Prentice Hall.

Brown, R. I. (1993). Quality of life issues in aging and intellectual disability. *Australia and New Zealand Journal of Developmental Disabilities, 18*(4), 219–227.

Brown, R. I., Bayer, M. B., and Brown, P. M. (1992). *Empowerment and developmental handicaps: Choices and quality of life*. Toronto: Captus Press.

Bullock, C. C. and Howe, C. Z. (1991). A model therapeutic recreation program for the reintegration of persons with disabilities into the community. *Therapeutic Recreation Journal, 25*(1), 7–17.

Bullock, C. C. and Luken, K. (1994). Recreation through reintegration. In D. Compton and S. E. Iso-Ahola, (Eds), *Leisure and mental health*. (pp. 215-233). Park City, UT: Family Development Resources.

Brissett, D. and Snow, R. P. (1993). Boredom: Where the future isn't. *Symbolic Interactionism, 16*(3), 237–256.

Caldwell, L. L., Smith, E. A., and Weissinger, E. (1992). The relationship of leisure activities and perceived health of college students. *Leisure and Society, 15*(2), 545–556.

Caldwell, L. L. and Smith, E. A. (1995). Health behaviors of leisure alienated youth. *Loisir et Societe: Leisure and Society, 18*, 149–156.

Dattilo, J. (1994). *Inclusive leisure services*. State College, PA: Venture Publishing, Inc.

Dattilo, J., Dattilo, A., Samdahl, D., and Kleiber, D. (1994). Leisure orientations and self-esteem in women with low incomes who are overweight. *Journal of Leisure Research, 26*(1), 23–38.

Datillo, J. and Murphy, W. (1991). *Leisure education program planning: A systematic approach*. State College, PA: Venture Publishing Inc.

Datillo, J. and St. Peter, S. (1991). A model for including leisure education in transition programs for young adults with mental retardation. *Education and Training in Mental Retardation, 26*, 420–432.

De Grazia, S. (1964). *Of time, work and leisure*. Garden City, NY: Anchor Books.

Glyptis, S. (1989). Leisure and unemployment. In E. J. Jackson and T. L. Burton (Eds.), *Understanding leisure and recreation: Mapping the past and charting the future* (pp. 151–180). State College, PA: Venture Publishing, Inc.

Haworth, J. and Evans, S. (1987). Meaningful activity and unemployment. In D. Fryer and Pullock (Eds.), *Unemployed people: Social and psychological perspectives* (pp. 241–267). Milton Keynes, UK: Open University Press.

Havitz, M. E. and Spigner, C. (1992). Access to public leisure services: a comparison of the unemployed with traditional target groups. *Journal of health, physical education, recreation and dance, 63*(4), 41–44.

Hepworth, S. J. (1980). Moderating factors of the psychological impact of unemployment. *Journal of Occupational Psychology, 53,* 139–145.

Hoge, G., Datillo, J., and Williams, R. (1999). Effects of leisure education on perceived freedom in leisure of adolescents with mental retardation. *Therapeutic Recreation Journal, 33*(4), 320–332.

Iso-Ahola, S. E. and Weissinger, E. (1990). Perceptions of boredom in leisure: Conceptualization, reliability and validity of the Leisure Boredom Scale. *Journal of Leisure Research, 22,* 1–17.

Jahoda, M. (1982). *Employment and unemployment: A social-psychological analysis.* Cambridge, UK: Cambridge University Press.

Kraus, R. (1994). Tomorrow's leisure: meeting the challenges. *The Journal of Physical Education, Recreation and Dance, 65*(4), 42–47.

Kraus, R. (2001). *Recreation and leisure in modern society.* (6th Edition), Boston: Jones and Bartlett.

Lobo, F. (1997). Young people, leisure and unemployment in Western Australia. *World Leisure and Recreation, 39*(4), 4-9.

Lobo, F. (2001). Unemployment, leisure and exclusion: challenges for equity and inclusion. In I. Patterson and T. Taylor (Eds.), *Celebrating inclusion and diversity in leisure* (pp. 147–160). Williamstown, Victoria: HM Leisure Planning.

Langer, E. J. and Rodin, J. (1976). The effects of choice and enhanced personal responsibility for the aged: A field experiment in an institutional setting. *Journal of Personality and Social Psychology, 34,* 191–198.

Larson, R., Mannell, R., and Zuzanek, J. (1986). Daily well-being of older adults with friends and family. *Journal of Psychology and Aging, 1,* 117–126.

Larson, R. W. and Richards, M. H. (1991). Boredom in the middle school years: Blaming schools versus blaming students. *American Journal of Education,* 418–443.

Lockwood, R., J., Lockwood, A. D., and O'Meara, W. (1991). Focus of change in leisure for people with disabilities. *Leisure Options: Australian Journal of Leisure and Recreation, 1,* 15–18.

McGill, J. (1996). *Developing leisure identities: A pilot project.* Ontario, Canada: Brampton Caledon Community Living.

McNeil, R. D. and Anderson, S. C. (1999). Leisure and persons with developmental disabilities: empowering self-determination through inclusion. In P. Retish and S. Reiter (Eds.), *Adults with disabilities: International perspectives in the community* (pp. 125–143). Mahwah, NJ: Lawrence Erlbaum Associates.

Mahon, M. J. and Searle, M. S. (1994). Leisure education: It effects on older adults. *Journal of Physical Education, Recreation, and Dance, 65*(4), 36–41.

Moos, R. H. (1989). Work as human context. In M. S. Pallak and R. Perloff (Eds.), *Psychology and work: Productivity, change and employment* (pps. 16–37). Washington, DC: American Psychological Association.

Mundy, J. (1998). *Leisure education: Theory and practice* (2nd edition). Chicago, IL: Sagamore.

Nour, K., Desrosiers, J., and Gauthier, P. (2002). Impact of a home based leisure education program for older adults who have had a stroke. *Therapeutic Recreation Journal, 36*(1), 48–66.

Patterson, I. R. (2000). Developing a meaningful identity for people with disabilities through serious leisure activities. *World Leisure Journal, 2,* 41–51.

Patterson, I. R. (2001). Serious leisure as a positive contributor to social inclusion for people with disabilities. *World Leisure Journal, 3,* 16–24.

Patterson, I. R., Pegg, S. A., and Dobson-Patterson, R. E. (2000). Exploring the links between leisure boredom and alcohol use among youth in rural and urban areas of Australia. *Journal of Park and Recreation Administration, 18*(3), 40–62.

Pesavento Raymond, L. C. (1992). Research in unemployment and leisure. *Parks and Recreation, 27*(6), 19–23, 83.

Roberts, K. (1997). Work and leisure in young people's lives. In J. T. Haworth (Ed.), *Work, leisure and well being* (pp. 143–164). London: Routledge.

Robinson, J. P. and Werner, P. (1997). Freeing up the golden years. *American Demographics, 19*(10), 20–23.

Rodin, J. and Langer, E. J. (1977). Long-term effects of a control-relevant intervention with the institutionalized aged. *Journal of Personality and Social Psychology, 35,* 897–902.

Schleien, S. J. and Ray, M. T. (1988). *Community recreation and people with disabilities: Strategies for integration*. Baltimore: Paul H. Brookes.

Searle, M. S., Mactavish, J. S., and Brayley, R. E. (1993). Integrating ceasing participation with other aspects of leisure behaviour: A replication and extension. *Journal of Leisure Research, 25*(4), 389–104.

Searle, M. S. and Mahon, M. J. (1991). Leisure education in a day hospital: The effects on selected social-psychological variables among older adults. *Canadian journal of community mental health, 10*(2), 95–109.

Searle, M. S., Mahon, M. J., Iso-Ahola, S. E., Sdrolias, H. A., and van Dyck, J. (1995). Enhancing a sense of independence and psychological well-being among the elderly: a field experiment. *Journal of Leisure Research, 27*(2), 107–124.

Shaw, S. M., Caldwell, L. L., and Kleiber, D. A. (1996). Boredom, stress and social control in the daily activities of adolescents. *Journal of Leisure Research, 28*(4), 274–292.

Simmons Market Research Bureau (1988). *The USA study of media and markets*. New York.

Stebbins, R. (1992). *Amateurs, professionals, and serious leisure*. Montreal: McGill-Queen's University Press.

Stebbins, R. (2000). Serious leisure for people with disabilities. In A. Sivan and H. Ruskin (Eds.), *Leisure education, community development and populations with special needs* (pp. 101–108). Oxford & New York: CABI Publishing.

Stebbins, R. (2001). Serious leisure. *Society, 38*(4), 53–57.

Tabourne, C. E. (1992). Name that tune: Leisure education with the elderly. *Parks and Recreation, 27*(4), 46–48, 82.

Verbrugge, L. M. (1990). The iceberg of disability. In S. M. Stahl (Ed.), *The legacy of longevity: Health and health care in later life* (pp. 55–75). Newbury Park, CA: Sage Publications.

Vodanovich, S. V., Verner, K. M., and Gilbride, T. V. (1991). Boredom proneness: Its relationship between positive and negative affect. *Psychological Reports, 69*, 1139–1146.

Warr, P. (1987). *Work, unemployment, and mental health*. Oxford, UK: Oxford University Press.

Wearing, B. and Wearing, S. (1988). All in a day's leisure: Gender and the concept of leisure. *Leisure Studies, 7*, 111–123.

Wegner, L., Flisher, A. J., Muller, M., and Lombard. C. (2006). Leisure boredom and substance use among high school students in South Africa. *Journal of Leisure Research, 38*(2), 249–266.

World Leisure and Recreation Association (2001). International position statement on leisure education and populations of special needs. *Leisure Sciences, 23,* 293–297.

Chapter Eight
Leisure Education and the
Leisure Industries
by Karla A. Henderson

A "leisure age" was forecast over 50 years ago. Concerns were raised at that time about whether people could handle leisure for their own good and for their communities. The idea that leisure was a commodity accessible for everyone was positive and yet problematic at the same time. Would people know how to use their leisure wisely? Technology was predicted to free people from hard physical work; computers would revolutionize the way work was done. The recognition that leisure could become a problem, however, led to the need to focus on the producers of positive structured and planned leisure opportunities (i.e., leisure industries comprising public and private providers who would assure that leisure would be handled appropriately). Free time could make for a higher quality of life for all, but those outcomes likely would not happen without a structure to enhance experiences through providing various individual, family, and community-based opportunities.

Although the dawn of the 21st century did not herald the leisure age, many people in the developed world have more leisure time than their parents, even though some are not satisfied with the amount and quality (Robinson and Godbey, 1999). Nevertheless, numerous leisure opportunities exist.

The most obvious way to promote positive leisure experiences is to provide activities that can be experienced, bought, and consumed. Therefore the commodity of leisure and the way that it is consumed or experienced relates to the product "sold." If people are not satisfied with their leisure, then perhaps the commodified opportunities are not what they desire. Perhaps more and better opportunities are needed that are not just diversionary, but offer opportunities for growth and self-efficacy.

The leisure industries that have evolved in industrialized countries over the past 50 to 75 years are based on the idea that people's demands for leisure create a supply of opportunities. Similarly, a supply of activities requires that demand be created. Thus, many private, public, sports-oriented, and tourist-based opportunities have been created for people seeking ways to consume, experience, and enjoy leisure. People develop awareness and appreciation of leisure in numerous ways, but in today's world a good deal of experiential learning comes from the promotion and marketing of activities by the various providers that comprise what is sometimes referred to as the leisure industries.

The purpose of this chapter is to highlight the means for providing leisure experiences and leisure education for individuals as well as communities through the work of a burgeoning group of leisure industries. The chapter is divided into a discussion of leisure education, the types of private and public leisure services and industries that exist, and specific aspects of sports and tourism as visibly growing leisure industries.

The author contends that in the broadest sense, all leisure industries contribute in one way or another toward leisure education.

Leisure Education

Leisure education is the foundation of this book, but the author will try to frame leisure education as a foundation for examining what leisure industries have to contribute. Fundamentally, when examining the importance of leisure and education, most Americans take their philosophy from John Dewey (1939) p. 1 who stated, "Perhaps the most deep-seated antithesis which has shown itself in education history is that between education in preparation for useful labor and education for a life of leisure." Education has the potential to draw all aspects of life together in the form of lifelong learning, leading to important work and meaningful leisure. Leisure is not "apart from" life but is "a part of" life. Therefore, leisure and education, in whatever form it takes, should contribute to just societies and edifying the lives of individuals in communities.

The connections between leisure and education have a number of broadly defined possibilities. Ideas linking education and leisure include "education for leisure," "education to leisure," "education through leisure," "education as leisure," "education during leisure," and "education about leisure." They represent somewhat similar meanings because they focus on the relationships possible between education and leisure. They also represent different approaches and highlight both the breadth and depth needed to understand leisure behavior. Leisure education can be both a subject and a context (American Association of Leisure and Recreation, 2003) for addressing the contribution of leisure to the quality of life for individuals and communities.

The history of leisure is also the history of informal education. Broadly defined, education is the process of giving instruction to impart knowledge, skills, and character building. Similarly, the outcomes of leisure in an idealistic way are to develop or embody knowledge, skills, and character. Education and leisure (i.e., recreation), in their best forms, are one and the same (Henderson, 1981). The history of leisure often begins with a discussion of the Greek philosophers with explicit empirical demarcation evident with the beginning of the Industrial Age. The history of leisure and education, however, has always been present since people first began to inhabit the earth in all cultures.

In the book of Genesis, Adam and Eve surely had all the leisure they wanted. The "curse" that God put on them was to toil instead of to leisure. Veal and Lynch (2001) described the historical and contemporary leisure of Aboriginal people related to how pleasure, satisfactions, and playfulness were, and continue to be, woven into and around the activities of everyday life. The more visible expressions of this leisure for indigenous people usually include games, talk, playfulness, storytelling, and art. The Eastern cultures in the Tao Te Ching also talk about a notion of leisure:

There is a time for being ahead,
a time for being behind;
a time for being in motion,
a time for being at rest;
a time for being vigorous,
a time for being exhausted;
a time for being safe,
a time for being in danger... Mitchell (translation, 1992, selection 29)

Many religions imply elements of leisure and recreation in their teachings (Kaza, 1996). For example, from Judaism, the concept of "Sabbath" is emphasized in letting the body rest. Christians stress notions of right action in all that people undertake. Islam focuses on remembrance and the importance of work and play experiences within the moral law. Hindus teach the value of karma and the law of cause and effect regarding any action. Buddhism focuses on the interdependence (i.e., yin-yang) of what people do (e.g., leisure-work). Thus, "Even though the word leisure is not known everywhere in the world, leisure is of all times, places and societies" (World Leisure International Centre of Excellence, 2005).

Arnold (1989) noted that Aristotle was the first to describe the relationship between leisure, education, and work, and he asked the question of whether the end of education is culture or whether it is to fit people for the business of life. From Aristotle's perspective, leisure did not denote rest or recreation, but was meant to be engaged in with the highest capacities of the soul. Arnold further suggested that notions of education as leisure are Aristotelian and connote meanings of liberal education.

Beyond a philosophical and historical discussion of education and leisure, the ideas are pragmatic, at least in the Western world, relative to the notions of education for, to, through, as, during, and about leisure, which I discuss in two categories of leisure education and professional education.

The Foundations of Leisure Education

Notions of leisure education are focused on improving the quality of life for individuals and communities. World Leisure (2005) typically has defined leisure education as primarily a subject in schools:

> The main aim of leisure education in educational frameworks is to help the individual, the family, the community, and the society to achieve a suitable quality of life and good health by using leisure time intelligently, by developing and cultivating physical, emotional, spiritual, mental, and social aspects, each individually or combined, as they relate to the aims of education in the country and its cultural heritage. (p. 4)

The author contends, however, that leisure education should and does occur in many other ways than through schools. The American Association of Leisure and Recreation (2003) described leisure education as potentially being the subject of leisure (e.g., education about, for, and to leisure) or leisure as the context of education (e.g., education through, during, and as leisure). The latter approach relates to informal and nonformal settings within leisure industries where education about, for, to, through, during, and as leisure occurs, whether consciously addressed or not.

Newer ideas about leisure education, including both subject and context, were evident, for example, in Liou's (2000) description of the need for leisure education in Taiwan. He suggested that the advanced development of the economy does not necessarily affect the quality of life for leisure in a country. Therefore, leisure education is not only necessary, but also urgent in terms of defining leisure, encouraging research, enhancing professional training, developing diverse programs of leisure activities for citizens, paying attention to the fairness and justice of leisure, and focusing on meeting the objectives of leisure for a country like

Taiwan. Another example of the growing interest in elements of leisure education is the World Exposition on Leisure, which showcases China's commitment to leisure as an essential element of its prominence in the global society (World Leisure Exposition, 2005).

The history of leisure education as a subject is relatively recent and has not been particularly successful in its initiation into schools. In 1987, Fragniere guest edited a special issue of *European Journal of Education* to focus on "education for leisure" (i.e., instead of education and leisure, education as leisure, or education during leisure) as integral to the role that leisure should play in people's lives. Fragniere presented this discussion of education for leisure with three foci: 1) the fundamental impact of leisure on the human condition, 2) curriculum content, and 3) the impact of education for leisure on institutional structures and policies. He noted that up to the mid-1980s, education was predicated on labor market demands. With the coming forecast of a "leisure society" this emphasis on work might not be as important as in the past. Corijn (1987) similarly advocated for leisure education as the complement to economic development. A variety of contrasting opinions about education for leisure were presented in this special issue. For example, Ruskin (1987) focused specifically on schools as the delivery mechanism for leisure education. Corijn concluded that education for leisure was not likely to occur in schools because, "it is likely that education for leisure will remain for the time being a fascinating intellectual challenge but a marginal social practice" (p. 273). Theeboom and Bollaert (1987) suggested that extracurricular activities (e.g., socio-cultural activities such as music and drama as well as sporting activities) associated with schools were the likely way that leisure education would occur, which they termed part of a utilitarian-adaptive approach (i.e., a contextual approach connoting integration without seeking it directly).

Corijn (1987) was right. The notion of leisure education as a subject has not become a mainstreamed "social practice" over the years despite attempts by several individuals and groups (e.g., American Association of Leisure and Recreation, 2003; Dattilo, 1999; Dattilo and Williams, 1999; Heyne and Schleien, 1996; Mundy, 1998; World Leisure, 2005) to address its importance to special groups as well as all citizens. However, it has been applied to particular populations. The solution to many of the problems associated with leisure is often to recommend "leisure education," which sometimes sounds like a cliché since that recommendation is so nonspecific.

Leisure education can also be addressed, perhaps more fruitfully, as a context. Aspects of education during, through, and as leisure reflect the informal connections between leisure and education. Mundy (1998) might refer to this approach as laissez-faire, but other professionals might argue that education is inherent in leisure participation in activities such as recess, after school programs, summer camps, sports leagues, tourism destinations, adult education programs, and any number of other opportunities where individuals have an opportunity to learn about and express themselves.

Recreation and leisure are learned experiences (Godbey, 1989). Some forms of leisure involve skills while others do not. People generally prefer doing leisure activities in which they feel competent. Thus, learning specific skills cannot be disassociated from the appreciation and enjoyment of experiences. People with higher levels of education often have more leisure skills because the process of education itself exposes them to various alternatives and "socializes" them into activities. Therefore, the availability and meanings of leisure opportunities vary greatly across cultures. Education for living through leisure can take numerous forms within social contexts. This education could include a focus on youth development as well as of healthy aging and applies across the lifespan. The context of leisure education has connections to "active learning" and "experiential education" that contribute to quality of life. Since the subject of leisure education has not gained widespread support, the context of leisure as education may be a focus for the future.

Whether leisure education is embodied formally or informally, leisure is a site where social, political, educational, and cultural relations are visible. Godbey (1989) described the numerous leisure contexts:

> Leisure behavior is an important consideration in the design of schools and public housing, the development of highway systems, in the well-being of the armed forces, the incarceration and rehabilitation of criminals, in the management of public institutions for various special populations, and, to some capacity, in almost every function of government. (p. 624)

Leisure's importance and value both as a subject and a context requires advocacy from citizens, professionals, nongovernmental organizations, and governmental entities. To use Coalter's (1999) comparison, an understanding of "society in leisure," (i.e., a contextual emphasis) and "leisure in society" (i.e., a focus on leisure as an element of life that has a unique role to play) are both needed in efforts to advocate for leisure. Leisure industries have provided this advocacy to various degrees.

Therefore, to understand the importance of leisure as well as how organizations and leisure industries provide a de facto opportunity for leisure education, I will describe briefly the role of professional education relative to leisure industries before turning to the various industries that contribute.

Professional Education

Professional education provides individuals and organizations with the skills and opportunities to facilitate leisure, recreation, tourism, and play experiences in a structured and organized fashion that are sometimes referred to as leisure industries. The first formal university programs in the United States that trained individuals to teach and lead recreation primarily within public agencies started in the 1930s. These professional programs grew relatively slowly until the 1960s, at which point they exploded in North America and other parts of the world such as Europe, Australia, and New Zealand. For example, Spain has had recreation training programs since 1960. Corijn (1987) described a curriculum developed in France by Dumazedier called animation. Dumazedier's program, initiated in the 1960s, was focused on how leaders could be trained to impart leisure education to participants. These emerging professional programs in the past 50 years focused on how society could develop institutions (e.g., public recreation centers, mass sporting events, tourism destinations) that would provide successful social, cultural, and economic approaches to providing leisure opportunities.

Professional and technical training educational opportunities generally occur in postsecondary schools and are part of both technical and/or university education. The purpose of this formal education was, and continues to be, to prepare individuals to manage areas, facilities, and programs that will offer recreation opportunities for people in all types of communities. The focus may be on parks, outdoor areas, tourist attractions, health institutions, or community programs. The venues might be governmental, not-for-profit, or private/commercial entities. The breadth of these possibilities and the professionalization of the field have grown steadily throughout the world in the past 50 years.

Although the author calls these early programs "professional education," the evolution of the field of leisure, recreation, and tourism management into leisure industries and as a profession continues to be a work in progress. Sessoms (1990) described six criteria that must be met before an area of service is considered a profession: an alliance with a social concern (i.e., the belief that professionals have in the value of recreation and leisure opportunities for the quality of individual and community life), professional societies and associations (e.g., World Leisure, Leisure Studies Association, Canadian Park and Recreation Association), a code of ethics, a specialized body of knowledge (i.e., research, which will be discussed later in this paper), professional education and training, and professional standards of accreditation, certification, and licensing.

The degree of professionalizing (i.e., according to Sessoms' 1990 criteria) varies throughout the world. Dustin and Goodale (1999) noted that more students are professionally educated (i.e., trained) in parks, recreation, and leisure studies in the United States than in all the other countries in the world combined. Professional standards such as accreditation (e.g., university curricula as well as agency practices) and certification (e.g., Certified Park and Recreation Professional) are primarily American approaches. Efforts in developing professional education programs, however, are gaining impetus throughout the world. As leisure industries evolve, they generally require some means for assuring that appropriate and ethically conducted opportunities are provided to consumers.

An example of efforts to provide higher education opportunities for individuals in countries that do not offer extensive professional training programs related to leisure industries is the World Leisure International Centre for Excellence (WICE) at Wageningen University in the Netherlands. The focus of this program is on leisure and the environment, with special attention on tourism. The current master's degree program has been offered by World Leisure for over 10 years to several hundred students with faculty from around the world. The program is designed to be an advanced, worldwide, transdisciplinary, critical, and innovative approach to an analysis of the significance and meanings of leisure choices in both consumption and production. Currently, WICE at Wageningen University, in cooperation with Valencia University in Spain, is creating a 4-year international bachelor-level educational program on "Leisure and the Environment" (World Leisure International Centre of Excellence, 2005). This pilot professional education initiative will be targeted to Latin American students and will be located in Uruguay. Other similar initiatives are in development, including projects in South Africa for African students, Nanjing and Hangzhou for students in China, and Jaipur, India for Indian students. The programs all aim to provide appropriate education to enhance leisure industries around the world.

Describing professional education and the foundation of leisure industries means that a plethora of activities might be addressed. The remainder of this chapter focuses on how leisure industries relate to one another to address the perceived needs and interests of individuals and communities.

The Myriad of Leisure Industries

Although professional education is not a prerequisite for being part of the leisure delivery industry and most leisure industry representatives do not specifically refer to their role in leisure education, many approaches are evident around the world. For purposes of this chapter, the author describes the leisure industry as it encompasses leisure and recreation pursuits comprised from three primary sectors: public (i.e., governmental), not-for-profit private (i.e., non-governmental organizations-NGOs), and commercial private (i.e., for-profit) sectors. Each has a somewhat unique mission, but all contribute together to provide leisure experiences. Over the past 100 years, they have paralleled one another in their evolution as an understanding of the importance of leisure and recreation has also evolved. Similarly, each confronts different but related challenges in the 21st century.

Figure 8.1 (on p. 140) provides a table adapted from Henderson et al. (2001) that shows the relationships between the elements of the three sectors.

Briefly, public leisure industries are governmentally supported and are theoretically available to all citizens of a community, region, or nation. Not-for-profit NGO's are usually focused on a particular activity or group of individuals and are limited based on the mission of the particular organization. Private commercial organizations are aimed at satisfying, and often creating, a demand for leisure services and are focused on appealing to participants (i.e., customers) who will purchase a product. Private leisure industries are probably the fastest growing sector because of the commodification of leisure and the market driven nature of the world's economy.

All sectors share the common focus of providing leisure, sports, recreation, arts, or tourism opportunities and experiences. They obviously differ in their philosophies, objectives, facilities, financing, and membership. Although a difference exists in the qualifications for leadership, each is concerned with providing quality leadership to reach the service and financial goals. Employees who cannot deliver the leisure product will likely not remain involved in the industry. The author will briefly discuss each of these three areas and then branch into other emerging forms of leisure industries that do not fall neatly into the tripartite traditional service delivery.

Public Recreation

Public recreation and the involvement of governments in leisure services stems from a concern for citizens' health and welfare and the use of

	PUBLIC	NOT-FOR-PROFIT	PRIVATE/COMMERCIAL
Philosophy of Service	Enrichment of the quality of life of the community by providing opportunities for the meaningful use of leisure.	Enrichment of the participating members by offering opportunities for meaningful use of leisure, frequently with emphasis on the group and individual.	Satisfying public demand for recreation experiences and services in an effort to produce profit.
Objectives of Service	To provide leisure opportunities that contribute to the social, physical, educational, cultural, and general well-being of the community.	To provide appealing activities to members that provide opportunities for close group association with an emphasis on human development, behavior, environmental, and social values.	To provide activities or programs that will appeal to customers. Seeks to meet competition and net a profit while serving the public.
Types of Agencies	Governmental units (federal, state, county, and local) such as park and recreation departments, recreation and park districts, and state park departments.	Boy Scouts, Girl Scouts, Camp Fire, "Y" organizations, tennis clubs, swim clubs, environmental organizations, and neighborhood recreation associations.	Corporations, franchises, partnerships, and private ownership such as resorts, theme parks, and professional sports.
Finance	Primarily by governmental support/taxes, but also by gifts, grants, trust funds, fees, and charges.	By gifts, grants, endowments, donations, fund-rasing drives, and membership fees.	By investment of the owner, and of promoters with users who pay admission and charges.
Facilities	Community buildings, parks (national, state, local), athletic fields, playgrounds, playfields, stadiums, camps, beaches, museums, zoos, and golf courses.	Community centers, youth centers, athletic facilities, play areas, environmental reserves, clubs, camps, and aquatic areas.	Theaters, clubs, taverns, night clubs, lounges, race tracks, bowling lanes, amusement parks, and stadiums.
Leadership	Professionally prepared individuals (preferably with leisure services background) provide and manage comprehensive recreation programs; uses volunteers as well as professionals.	Educated individuals to provide programs, frequently on a social group-work basis; uses many volunteers as well as professionals.	Business and sales-oriented personnel to design and manage services to produce a profit, in compliance with state and local laws.
Membership	Unlimited and open to all.	Limited by organization's mission, such as age, gender, or religion.	Limited generally by economics to those participants who pay for the service or product.

FIGURE 8.1 Relationships Between the Elements of the Three Sectors

natural resources (Henderson et al., 2001). Democratic and representative governments have the responsibility to provide a respectable quality of life that is available for all citizens.

Four basic functions are evident in the provision of leisure opportunities from a public governmental perspective. The first is the management of land and natural resources. A typical aspect of this management is the provision of opportunities for outdoor recreation while simultaneously assuring that the resources are not exploited. In the United States, federal and state governments have focused primarily on resource-oriented outdoor recreation, while local governments have provided both resource and activity oriented opportunities.

A second function of public leisure providers is to provide technical and financial assistance in the form of information as well as potentially grant-funding. A third responsibility is direct service delivery in the form of activity instruction, competition, special events, and performances. Finally, public recreation providers are often responsible for enacting and enforcing regulations surrounding recreation through enabling and regulatory laws.

As noted earlier, the roots of the recreation movement were focused on public recreation. With the growing recognition of people's needs for recreation and leisure opportunities, other sectors became involved. In many countries, these sectors work together well in fulfilling their unique missions and in forming partnerships with one another. In some countries where an infrastructure of public recreation was never in place, the not-for-profit and private sectors have been responsible for addressing the leisure needs of citizens as well as visitors.

Not-for-Profit Organizations

Not-for-profit organizations (i.e., nonprofit, voluntary, third sector, independent sector, or nongovernmental organizations-NGOs) are voluntary associations that focus on a particular issue, activity, or population. Most of these organizations receive support in a number of ways, including membership fees, donations, grants, fundraising endeavors, and sometimes limited governmental backing.

Salamon (1999) described a number of reasons why the not-for-profit sector should exist. First, local groups often identify needs within their communities before governments can react. These organizations also exist to address these needs either on a membership basis (e.g., YMCA, Girls Scouts/Girl Guides, sports leagues) or as a means for public service (e.g., environmental groups such as Sierra Club, health-related groups such as Diabetes Association, or religious groups). Many of these organizations interests overlap between their members, social justice, and advocacy. Many not-for-profit groups employ professional staff, but the bulk of work is often done by volunteers. Some of these NGOs operate solely to provide recreation, sport, and leisure opportunities. Other not-for-profit groups exist for many reasons with leisure and recreation being only one aspect. However, in many communities the provision of recreation opportunities, especially in the form of sports and arts involvement, is offered to a great extent solely because of these not-for-profit groups. Youth services as not-for-profit entities, in particular, are common in many parts of the world.

Private Businesses

Private or commercial recreation is a growing sector, with new markets, services, and products appearing almost daily. About seven percent of the total consumption of goods and services in the United States is attributed to recreation, with much of it being produced through private provision and marketing. Even though leisure goods may be exchanged, not all commercial providers may see themselves as part of the leisure industry. Nevertheless, they offer services that contribute to leisure and provide an informal means for leisure education in numerous ways.

The structures of these private commercial organizations vary from small industries such as a souvenir shop run by a single owner to multinational corporations (e.g., hotel chains, amusement parks). Bullaro and Edginton (1986) developed a scheme to describe five service domains within the private sector: entertainment services (e.g., bowling alleys, circuses, rodeos, waterparks), natural resource-based services (e.g., campgrounds, marinas, ski resorts, wildlife parks), retail outlets (e.g., shopping malls, dance studios, golf courses, fitness clubs), hospitality and food services (e.g., hotels, resorts, convention centers), and travel and tourism services (e.g., tour promoters, travel agencies).

This private sector of the leisure industry is huge, providing many opportunities for investment and profit making for entrepreneurs. Because of the competitive nature of this sector, these industries are always focused on improvement to attract participants. Satisfied customers will return as well as tell their friends about the good leisure experience. The more positive experiences that people have, the more they are likely to seek those types of experiences in the future.

Other Related Leisure Industries

Other areas of leisure-related industries exist that are not directly linked to the direct service provisions of public, not-for-profit, and private leisure industries. The author will briefly mention these since they are not necessarily directly focused on providing leisure experiences per se, and yet they contribute immensely to how people use their time. Many of these leisure-related areas also cross-cut with other purposes.

Examples of this leisure-related sector might also be referred to as "edutainment." Edutainment (i.e., educational entertainment or entertainment-education) is a form of entertainment designed to educate as well as to amuse (Nahrstedt, 2000;Wikipedia, 2006a). Edutainment typically seeks to instruct or socialize its audience by embedding lessons in some familiar form of entertainment, such as television programs, computer and video games, films, music, websites, or multimedia software.

Edutainment often seeks to change behavior by engendering specific sociocultural attitudes. Various groups in the United States and the United Kingdom have used edutainment to address such health and social issues as substance abuse, immunization, teenage pregnancy, HIV/AIDS, and cancer. Edutainment defines some children's television series such as *Sesame Street*, *Dora the Explorer*, and *Teletubbies*. For some older viewers, individual situation comedy episodes also occasionally serve as edutainment vehicles. For example, one episode of the American sitcom *Happy Days* was reported to have prompted a 600 percent increase in demand for library cards in the United States (Wikipedia, 2006a). Meanwhile, the British radio soap opera *The Archers* has been systematically educating its audience on agricultural matters for decades. Similarly the Tanzanian radio soap opera *Twende na Wakati* ("Let's Go With the Times") was written primarily to promote family planning. Other examples of how leisure serves as a form of education through edutainment might be educational computer games, educational toys, and infomercials or infotainment.

Serious games (Wikipedia, 2006b) are computer and video games that are intended to not only entertain users, but to educate and train as well. A serious game is usually a simulation that has the look and feel of a game, but is actually a simulation of real-world events or processes that train or educate users. The game may also have other purposes such as marketing or advertisement, while giving players an enjoyable experience. Serious games can be of any genre, and many of them can be considered a kind of edutainment; however, the goal is not solely to entertain. Entertainment encourages re-use.

Therefore, leisure-related activities such as elements of popular culture (e.g., music, films, television, Internet) as edutainment might be considered important ways that people engage in leisure aside from structured leisure industries. Clearly, the opportunities for employment as well as participation in a variety of leisure education opportunities are huge. Two major areas related to leisure opportunities are sports and tourism.

Sports and Tourism Industries

Sports and tourism are probably the fastest growing of the industries, so I discuss them separately with limited detail. Sports refers to recreation activities that involve skills or physical prowess, generally of a competitive nature. Tourism refers most basically to traveling for pleasure. An emerging area also described is sport tourism.

Tourism

Tourism as an industry has gained acceptance and predominance in the past 50 years. Although travel for trade and religious purposes dates back to ancient times, tourism is a recent idea. Its growth as a major economic force and as a leisure opportunity for millions of people is due to both technological advances and affluence (Henderson et al., 2001). It is an outgrowth of people's desire to relax, to have new and different experiences away from their daily routines, to visit other environments, and to learn about other cultures.

Tourism, like other areas of the leisure industry, has numerous facets. It is often associated with recreation activities as well as with other service and hospitality businesses. Similarly, notions of travel and tourism are sometimes considered together, although travel may be done for many reasons other than tourism. Typically, tourism is based on the elements of distance traveled, motives of travel, and time required for the visit (Henderson et al., 2001). The distance traveled before an individual is classified as a tourist varies. Time spent away may also be misleading and often is associated with distance traveled. The reason for the trip might be one of the best ways to discern whether or not tourism is occurring. Nevertheless, one might be a tourist if he or she goes to an art museum in a community that is 50 miles away if one freely choose to go with the purpose of some type of intrinsic experience related to enjoyment. If that person stayed long enough to enjoy his or her choice, that person would be considered a tourist.

The economic and social impact of tourism is of growing significance. The tourism industry is worth trillions of dollars with an estimated $5.5 trillion U.S. generated in 2005 (Henderson et al., 2001). In addition, millions of people are employed in the industry. Governments and the tourism industry must work together to assure controlled growth and development and to minimize host community and visitor conflicts. Mass tourism is evident with the amount of money and time that is now available for large segments of people to participate. More affluence in economies has generated more tourism.

A number of factors influence tourism, including speed of travel, infrastructures, marketing, freedom of movement, and climate. With the speed of transportation, people can fly thousands of miles in a short period of time. However, a tourism attraction must be able to accommodate people with infrastructures that support the tourism, such as airports, restaurants, accommodations, and transportation systems. Marketing is essential to promote tourism relative to the location, natural resources, or attractions, such as cultural events and activities. Freedom of movement also contributes to tourism, especially international tourism. The global impact of terrorism as well as the open doors of previously Iron Curtain countries attests to issues related to the importance of perceptions of movement and tourism. Climate and climatic change also influence where people go and what their experience is.

The tourism industry faces a number of challenges for the future (Henderson et al., 2001). One issue relates to how much regulation of tourism should occur by governments as opposed to the industry itself. Another issue is the influence of tourism on the destination's social system and culture. Although tourism can be a huge boost to economically depressed areas, it also carries issues related to pollution, infrastructure costs, social problems, and potential seasonal unemployment. For example, tourism can negatively transform local cultures from a focus on the values and interests of the community to a reflection of the market.

Finally, tourism can have a negative impact on the environment. If the environment degrades, many forms of tourism change. Sustainable tourism is an approach that moves away from a strictly socioeconomic focus toward a focus on preserving resources for the future (Fennell, 1999). Sustainable tourism means not consuming natural resources at a higher rate than they can be replaced. Maintaining biological diversity, recognizing the aesthetic appeal of the environment, respecting local cultures, and consulting local people (Williams, 1998) are necessary for tourism to remain sustainable. Ecotourism is an emerging area that connects tourism to the environment. Ecotourism is focused on low impact, small-scale, nature-focused tourism that educates the traveler. The future of sustainable tourism, according to Fennell, is not only to bring a small number of environmentally conscious people into pristine environments, but to improve the sustainability of ethical and responsible mass tourism.

Despite the potential costs, tourism is likely to increase in popularity. Tourism affects almost everyone, whether producing, consuming, or living/traveling in cities or the countryside. Sustainable tourism can be maximized when all leisure industries work together to provide quality recreation opportunities. Tourism activities influence the quality of life of all individuals.

Sports Industries

The breadth of sports industries is also huge. Sports are typically defined as involving rules, requiring physical prowess, and including some form of competition. Since sport is generally freely chosen, it is considered an aspect of the leisure industry and ranges from international sporting events, such as the Olympics, to local sporting events. Further, not only are sports a means for participation, but they are also a venue for spectators. Veal and Lynch (1996) described sport as active participation as well as active or passive viewing.

Forsyth (2005) discussed the relationship of leisure, sport, and recreation as symbiotic. What differentiates sport from some other recreation activities are the emphasis on winning, extrinsic rewards, and the amount of structure or bureaucratization. He noted that recreation activities tend to evolve into organized opportunities (e.g., skateboarding by children in playgrounds evolved into a competitive opportunity; rock climbing was once only an outdoor activity but now is sometimes highly competitive and may be done indoors). These examples further illustrate the pervasive and changing nature of sports.

Historically, sports have had a variety of benefits and meanings. They are a means for reinforcing the values and identity of a culture. Sports provide ways for people to learn lifelong skills that enable them to be happier and healthier. Further, sports have a significant economic impact when one considers the amount of money spent in sports viewing as well as the cost of equipment and facilities for sport participation.

Sports can be organized in a number of ways. They may be the purview of public recreation providers such as through youth sports in city recreation leagues, the result of club activities generally sponsored by nongovernmental organizations, or they might be made available through private sports facilities that charge entrance fees. Sports activities cut across all sectors of the leisure industries.

Sports offer many opportunities for positive benefits but also have some drawbacks. For example, sports have traditionally been male dominated. Notions of what it means to be male or female within the wider culture have been reflected in the subcultures and structures of sports.

Women have often had to struggle against the male origins of sports, even though today women across the world are involved in many types of athletic endeavors. Another drawback related to sports spectatorship is crowd disorder. Unruly behavior, whether related to athlete behavior or among sports crowds, is an issue that provides some drawbacks to the benefits of the endeavors.

A rapidly growing area of the leisure related work force is sports management. Skills are needed to deal with the maintenance of facilities and the marketing of activities that comprise the wide range of sports opportunities. Some sports organizations deal with multi-million dollar budgets, but many small business operations occur in competitive markets that require business management skills such as marketing, accounting, personnel management, communications, and familiarity with law.

Sport Tourism

Sport tourism is a fast growing area within the leisure industries that combines sports and tourism. Many people travel to be a spectator or to participate in athletic events in nearby communities as well as around the world (e.g., Olympics). It is an increasingly popular tourism product that may take place in urban or nonurban settings, indoors or outdoors, in all types of climatic conditions, and in all seasons (Kurtzman and Zauhar, 2003). Interestingly, people have engaged in sport-related travel for centuries (Gibson, 1998). However, in the past ten years, its popularity has increased dramatically.

Sport tourism has a number of definitions. Sometimes it is referred to as sport(s) tourism and sometimes as tourism sport. The commonality exists in that it involves travel away from home to observe or participate in sport. Kurtzman and Zauhar (2003) suggested five core products of sport tourism: attractions (e.g., sports facilities such as stadiums and arenas), resorts (e.g., sites for sport activities), cruises (e.g., opportunities for sport involvement on board or at destinations), tours (specific planned group visits to museums, theme parks, major sporting events), and events (e.g., visits to sporting events). Gibson (1998) suggested that the three primary domains of sport tourism are active sport tourism (i.e., people who travel to take part in a sport), event sport tourism (i.e., travel to watch a sport), and nostalgic sport tourism (i.e., visits to sports museums, famous sports venues, and sports-themed cruises).

Similar to any area of recreation, sport tourism can have both positive and negative impacts (Higham, 2006). Sport tourism contributes to economic development, positive image and identity, and tourism promotion and marketing. On the opposite side, mega events can have short-term benefits but long-term consequences in terms of their costs. Increasingly, small scale sport tourism opportunities are being encouraged because they offer benefits for participants as well as local communities without major infrastructure consequences.

Summary

This chapter highlights the numerous possibilities for enhancing opportunities and educating about leisure through a plethora of leisure industries. In summary, three assumptions about leisure education provide some basis for future leisure advocacy and opportunity development. First, leisure is a part of life and extends from the play of children all the way to aging well. The basis for support for leisure opportunities is the belief (i.e., philosophy) and evidence (i.e., theory) that leisure can be a creative and constructive force in the lives of individuals, social groups, communities, and the global society. In this way, action is needed to ascertain and communicate the economic, social, and environmental potential of leisure and to provide a variety of opportunities for leisure expression.

Second, the relationship between leisure and education is multi-faceted. Education about, for, and to leisure cannot be disconnected contextually from education through, during, and as leisure. Numerous public, private, and personal opportunities exist for leisure that can empower individuals and develop healthy communities. Education related to leisure can provide recreation skills and decision-making processes for individuals as well as address leisure's social and environmental contributions to active citizenship and just societies.

Third, leisure is culturally situated with varying individualistic and collective manifestations that vary from country to country as well as within the diversity of a single country. One way to summarize the call to continued advocacy for leisure and education is to examine the "International Charter for Leisure" (World Leisure, 2005). These statements go directly to the heart of why leisure industries are important. Although the Charter specifically describes the role that governments should play, these items also reflect opportunities that are available for all aspects of leisure industries:

1. All people have a basic human right to leisure activities... All governments are obliged to recognize and protect this right of its citizens.
2. Governments should ensure their citizens a variety of accessible leisure and recreational opportunities of the highest quality.

3. Governments should ensure the means for acquiring the skills and understanding necessary to optimize leisure experiences.
4. Individuals can use leisure opportunities for finding self-fulfillment, developing personal relationships, improving social integration, and developing communities and cultural identity as well as promoting international understanding and enhancing quality of life.
5. Governments should ensure the future availability of fulfilling leisure experiences by maintaining the quality of the country's physical, social, and cultural environment.
6. Governments should ensure the training of professionals to help individuals acquire personal skills, discover and develop their talents, and broaden their range of leisure and recreational opportunities.
7. Citizens must have access to all forms of leisure information about the nature of leisure and its opportunities, and they should use this information to enhance their knowledge and inform decisions on local and national policy.
8. Educational institutions must make every effort to teach the nature and importance of leisure and how to integrate this knowledge into personal lifestyle.

The opportunities and challenges for leisure education are clearly linked to all leisure providers and consumers including citizens, professionals, educators, businesspeople, other stakeholders, and policy makers who believe in the value of leisure, recreation, sport, tourism, and play.

References

American Association of Leisure and Recreation (2003). *Leisure education in the schools: Taskforce on leisure education in the schools.* Reston, VA: American Alliance for Health, Physical Education, Recreation, and Dance.

Arnold, P. (1989). On the relationship between education, work and leisure: Past, present and future. *British Journal of Educational Studies, 37*(2), 136–146.

Bullaro, J. and Edginton, C. (1986). *Commercial leisure services: Managing for profit.* New York: McMillan.

Coalter, F. (1999). Leisure sciences and leisure studies: The challenge of meaning. In E. L. Jackson and T. L. Burton (Eds.), *Leisure studies: Prospects for the twenty-first century* (pp. 507–522). State College, PA: Venture Publishing, Inc.

Corijn, E. (1987). Leisure education and emancipation in today's context. *European Journal of Education, 22*(3/4), 265–274.

Dattilo, J. (1999). *Leisure education program planning: A systematic approach* (2nd edition). State College, PA: Venture Publishing.

Dattilo, J. and Williams, R. (1999). Inclusion and leisure service delivery. In E. L. Jackson and T. L. Burton (Eds.), *Leisure studies: Prospects for the twenty-first century* (pp. 451–463). State College, PA: Venture Publishing, Inc.

Dewey, J. (1939). *Democracy and education.* Retrieved October 26, 2007, from http://etext.lib.virginia.edu/etcbin/toccer-new2?id=DewDemo. sgm&images=images/modeng&data=/texts/english/modeng/parsed &tag=public&part=85&division=div2

Dustin, D. L. and Goodale, T. L. (1999). Reflections on recreation, park, and leisure studies. In E. L. Jackson and T. L. Burton (Eds.), *Leisure studies: Prospects for the twenty-first century* (pp. 477–486). State College, PA: Venture Publishing, Inc.

Fennell, D. A., (1999). *Ecotourism.* London: Routledge.

Fragniere, G. (1987). Editorial (for special issue on Education for Leisure). *European Journal of Education, 22*(3/4), 217-223.

Forsyth, C. J. (2005). Discerning the symbiotic relationship between sport, leisure, and recreation: A note on the sportization of pastimes. *Sociological Spectrum, 25,* 127–131.

Gibson, H. J. (1998). Sport tourism: A critical analysis of research. *Sport Management review, 1,* 45–76.

Godbey, G. (1989). Implications of recreation and leisure research for professionals. In E. L. Jackson and T. L. Burton (Eds.), *Understanding leisure and recreation: Mapping the past, charting the future* (pp. 613–628). State College, PA: Venture Publishing, Inc.

Henderson, K. A. (1981). A converging view of leisure and education. *Lifelong Learning: The Adult Years, 5*(12), 6–8.

Henderson, K. A., Bialeschki, M. D., Hemingway, J. L., Hodges, J. S, Kivel, B. D., and Sessoms, H. D. (2001). *Introduction to recreation and leisure services* (8th edition). State College, PA: Venture Publishing, Inc.

Heyne, L. A. and Schleien, S. J. (1996). Leisure education in the schools: A call for action. Journal of Leisurability, 23(3). Retrieved April 6, 2005, from http://www.lin.ca/resource/html/Vol23/v23n3a2.htm

Higham, J. (2006). Commentary—Sport as an avenue of tourism development: An analysis of positive and negative impacts of sports tourism. Retrieved on May 23, 2006 from http://divcom.otago. ac.nz:800/tourism/current-issues/homepage.htm

Kaza, S. (1996). Comparative perspectives on world religions: Views of nature and implications for land management. In B. L. Driver et al., *Nature and the human spirit* (pp. 41–60). State College, PA: Venture Publishing, Inc.

Kurtzman, J. and Zauhar, J. (2003). A wave in time—The sports tourism phenomena. *Journal of Sport Tourism, 8,* 35–47.

Liou, T. (2000). The study of leisure education in Taiwan (article written in Chinese). *Bulletin of Adult and Continuing Education, 29,* 221–247. English abstract retrieved April 6, 2005, from http://www. fed.cuhk.edu.hk/ceric/bse/200000290000/0221

Mitchell, S. (1992). *Tao te ching* (pocket edition). New York: HarperCollins.

Mundy, J. (1998). *Leisure education: Theory and practice* (2nd edition). Champaign, IL: Sagamore Publishing.

Nahrstedt, W. (2000). Global edutainment: The role of leisure education for community development. In A. Sivan and H. Ruskin, *Leisure education, community development, and populations with special needs* (pp 65–74). London: CAB International.

Robinson, J. P. and Godbey, G. (1999). *Time for life: The surprising ways Americans use their time* (2nd edition). University Park, PA: Pennsylvania State University Press.

Ruskin, H. (1987). A conceptual approach to education for leisure. *European Journal of Education, 22*(3/4), 281–290.

Salamon, L. M. (1999). *America's nonprofit sector: A primer.* New York: Foundation Center.

Sessoms, H. D. (1990). On becoming a profession: Requirements and strategies. *Journal of Park and Recreation Administration, 8*(4), 47–58.

Theeboom, M. and Bollaert, L. (1987). Leisure education and the school. *European Journal of Education, 22*(3/4), 299–308.

Veal, A. J. and Lynch, R. (2001). *Australian leisure* (2nd edition). Frenchs Forest, NSW: Longman.

Wikipedia. (2006a). Retrieved May 9, 2006, from http://en.wikipedia.org/wiki/Edutainment

Wikipedia (2006b). Retrieved May 9, 2006, from http://en.wikipedia.org/wiki/Serious_game

Williams, S. (1998). *Tourism geography.* London: Routledge.

World Leisure Exposition. (2005). Retrieved December 21, 2005, from http://www.worldleisure.org/expo2006/overview/html

World Leisure International Centre of Excellence (2005). Retrieved December 28, 2005, from http://www.wice.info/index5.htm

World Leisure. (2005). Retrieved December 19, 2005, from http://www.worldleisure.org

Chapter Nine
Conclusions
by Elie Cohen-Gewerc and Robert A. Stebbins

In our view, leisure education is a main route to enriching the lives of people whose leisure lifestyle is felt by them to be too uninteresting, unexciting, or incomplete or, for many harried people, nonexistent. In other words, when it comes to improving the human condition, leisure education has a pivotal role to play in reaching that goal. Moreover, the time to pursue that goal is now, with the amount of free time slowly expanding (for many people) and the disenchantment with both modern work and unpleasant nonwork obligations growing at an even faster rate. Put otherwise, the twenty-first century belongs to leisure education, and this book is our manifesto for advancing its cause.

Leisure education, as the preceding chapters demonstrate, offers much for children and adolescents, middle-aged and retired adults, people with disabilities, and those who are unemployed. For example, through leisure education, people gain opportunities to explore new interests as well as previously unknown aspects of themselves. The ancient Greek philosophers focused mostly on work (with a little time set aside for writing on recreation), in an era largely dedicated to examining the needs of life in what was essentially a search for meaning as related to survival and a variety of very practical concerns. By contrast, in this new century, humankind now feels a stirring of its own aspirations, undiluted by life's obligations. It is not enough simply to live in this new, open, and fertile world; we must try to identify and realize new interests and learn how to realize these aspirations. Thus, leisure education must include a reconceptualization of such ideas as time, risk, freedom, adventure, socialization, uncertainty, and above all, education itself. In other words education is far more than training people for work, in general, and an occupational role, in particular. Education also introduces people to a more intimate encounter between self and life in the comprehensive sense.

Summing Up

The upshot of this is that education can no longer be regarded as limited to a period of fifteen or even twenty years. All the chapters in this book make this point, each in its own way. Education must be conceived of more broadly as including lifelong, often self-directed, learning. Leisure education, in particular, becomes critical when we consider, for instance, the growing allure of the multitude of leisure industries and the often-times weak market skills of consumers as they attempt to choose among them. This is a worldwide issue, however, unlike the previously mentioned problem of lifelong and self-directed learning that is more or less unique to the West, where some people have so much free time that, to maximize benefits to self and community, they need leisure education to inform their use of it.

Our aim in this book has been to weave together, on a world scale, the main strands of this manifesto on leisure education, aided by a group of internationally recognized experts in this field. Our principal audience has been the leisure educators themselves (as defined above), researchers in the area, and leisure service providers, as well as students in leisure education and leisure provision. Still, educators of every stripe can, conceivably, also be interested in what has been said on these pages, as can some of the general public, whatever their age or walk of life. For it is among the general public that we find the "clients" of the leisure educator, the people who benefit from that expert's knowledge and experience.

The authors started, in chapter 1, with an overview of the serious leisure perspective and consideration of how leisure education fits within it. This perspective, particularly one of its three forms, serious leisure, found its way into the theoretic background of nearly every subsequent chapter. Chapter 3 centered on the nature of leisure education itself, and the central role that serious leisure plays there.

Chapter 3 needed further grounding, however, particularly in the social milieu within which leisure education takes place. That grounding was provided in chapter 2. Leisure in everyday life has, as Rojek observed in this chapter, real consequences for social capital and, by this avenue, the effective functioning of democracy. He introduces the idea of "neat capitalism": a type of market organization that recognizes ethical responsibilities at the levels of both the business corporation and the individual consumer. Elsewhere he (Rojek, 2002, pp. 26–27) argues that, for the most part, civil labor or community involvement constitutes an important contribution to community that amateurs, hobbyists, and career volunteers make when they pursue their serious leisure. Civil labor, however conceived of, generates social capital, defined here as the connections among individuals manifested in social networks, trustworthiness, acts motivated by the norm of reciprocity, and the like that develop in a community or larger society (Putnam, 2000, p. 19). The term is an analogy to the concepts of human capital and physical capital (e.g., natural resources, financial resources); it emphasizes that human groups of all kinds also benefit from and advance their interests according to the salutary interconnections of their members.

Yet, serious leisure, as a set of activities to undertake in free time, is neither well-known nor well-understood by the general population. This is one of the main reasons for offering leisure education. Unfortunately such education is not a process that can be carried off with ease. For we have seen in chapter 4 that, for children, educating for leisure is as complicated and challenging as educating for anything else. As evidence of this observation, Sivan described five subsystems affecting the ways the child operates with reference to leisure-related matters. They are the microsystem (direct personal contacts), the mesosystem (links between roles and structures in the microsystem), the exosystem (the larger circle of the social system in which the child has no direct involvement, but is nonetheless affected), the macrosystem (the culture guiding the first three subsystems), and the chronosystem (the changes over time in children's lives).

In chapter 5, Spector adds detail to this statement through her presentation of the results from two studies—one on children, the other on adolescents—as these groups pursue leisure though learning, free choice learning, and lifelong learning. The point of all three forms of learning is decidedly not economic; rather, it is developmental. Their aim is to foster personal growth, evident in, for example, enhanced individual identity, self-fulfillment, and sense of group or community accomplishment, as these are realized through serious leisure.

This interest in personal growth is also central in adult education and lifelong learning from mid-life through old age, as chapter 6 clearly demonstrates. There, Lobo focuses on working people in mid-life and older individuals after they cease paid employment. He observes that preparation for life during and after work not only aids developing a more satisfying lifestyle, but also helps achieve a balance in life across the lifespan. The key to optimal adjustment is through leisure, he said; more specifically, serious leisure within the disposition and framework of lifelong learning. His chapter suggested ways of aging well, and recommended approaches for personal development and further learning.

Staying with this theme of personal growth, Patterson explored the role of leisure education for people with disabilities and people who are unemployed in chapter 7. He noted that our culture devalues those who are not working, and as a result of this depreciation, they are less likely to fill valued social roles. He discussed the importance of leisure education in the lives of people who have special needs, proposing that governments and service delivery agencies place greater emphasis on leisure education programs that support the pursuit of serious leisure; that is, they should do more than merely provide diversionary, or time filling, casual leisure activities. A proper leisure education program provides skills, engenders confidence, and fosters abilities, thereby raising competency in future serious lifetime pursuits. For many people with special needs, open employment may not be a realistic option. For this reason, their lives may be boring and empty—unless, of course, serious leisure can be harnessed to provide them with the social role competencies and benefits that are similar to those achievable in the fulfilling forms of employment.

However, the provision of services is itself a complicated arena. Henderson observed in chapter 8 that the most obvious way to promote leisure is as a set of activities that can be observed, bought, consumed, or experienced. Therefore, leisure can also be understood as a commodity, and the way it is consumed or experienced relates to the product being sold. Leisure industries are based on the idea that the demand for leisure should create a supply of opportunities. People develop a complicated awareness and appreciation of leisure, but in today's world, a good deal of this learning comes through the promotion and marketing of leisure activities by the various providers.

The New Meaning of Leisure

In opposition to common terminology, by using "free time" and "leisure" as synonyms, the authors stress the difference in meaning between free time, which is time freed by external and changing circumstances independent of one's will, and leisure, which is an emanation of an inner, conscious state of mind. Today an inexorable process can be observed where free time, on one hand, becomes larger because of technological progress and its social consequences, but disappears, on the other hand, in the black hole of innumerable solicitations of consumption. When time is only a gap left empty by the lack of obligations, it means we have not yet reached our potential freedom.

There is time that often embarrasses people who, in part or in whole, were ejected out of their routine when roles that determined life's rhythm, or worse, legitimacy, disappeared. We have to remember that we live, at the beginning of this century, in the painful transition between the sinking era of work and the rising era of leisure, where we experience many negative effects.

Shakespeare wrote that "all the world's a stage." We can inspire ourselves from this observation to illustrate the Era of Work, which makes more and more room for an age we will call in a first approach, vis-à-vis the Era of Free Time, which can evolve, thanks to a new conception of education, into the Era of Leisure. In the conceptual approach of the era of work, the whole existence is a stage. That is, there is a clear distribution of tasks filling almost the whole temporal space of the individual. It is a role distribution which meshes with the wheels of society and its "written texts" for almost every temporal space.

People are socialized—they internalize the diverse elements of their society's culture (values, myths, symbols, narratives, norms, rules, etc.)—and feel tied to all roles they must fill. Going from one function to another, people perceive themselves only through these roles, in their respective order, and in the temporal space they are fully attached to. In such a context, we can never really speak of free time. All that exists of it are some intervals given to children to burn the excess energy compressed during their passive stay in class and given to adults to restore the energy wasted at work.

Defined roles and fixed schedules to be fulfilled mostly in the public spaces in which people are framed, have been, in all eras, the very foundation of social order. This includes the effective authority at all levels, starting with the family and including the entire society as well as all working places, religious institutions, and even established entertainment spaces.

Let us examine the framework of a homogeneous community, ruled by a set of internalized beliefs and the distribution of canonical roles. Here one of the chief means of every authority is to appropriate temporal space, making it cyclical like the passing of the seasons (Bergson, 1932), with a rigid and detailed timetable from dawn to dusk, from birth to death. In this scenario public events are numerous and pivotal for both group cohesion and voluntary, enthusiastic exercise of vigilance. The common prayer, practiced several times a day, is a kind of convocation where everyone cares and supervises the participation of other members, just as they take care and pressure the individual. In this form of society there is little room for maneuver, which is considered dangerous in the same way that freedom between pieces of any mechanism can endanger good performance (as established by the manufacturer's norms).

We can understand how technological improvement seen in shorting time and distances dramatically helps enlarge ever more the spaces we will call, as a first phase, spaces free from defined obligations and established roles. To sense the stress this process generates, it is enough to follow the efforts demanded by young parents who try tirelessly to find a new program, a new supervised activity, in which they can put their children for all the empty hours where they risk being alone. Here they play outside the wheels of regulation in the hazardous hands of free-time emptiness.

Another crucial aspect is the change occurring in what was the deep meaning of the function of work during the last two centuries. Work gives the individual a lot of central attributes: identity, security, continuity, and meaningful life, all of which revolve mostly around the occupational axis. Though, hardly anyone sees himself/herself occupying, in the distant future, the same position he/she occupies now, everyone is concerned about uncertainty, even those in the highest positions. Nobody is immune to this fragility in employment, which springs from the inherent fragility of firms themselves. Who could think, two decades ago, that a national company like Swissair—one Switzerland's symbols—could collapse and disappear, condemning thousands of people to unemployment, to forced free time? Even in administration the trend is to abolish the concept of tenure.

Free time is growing but so is the sense of emptiness, which is becoming a feature of life that most people try hard to ignore and escape through the incoherent distractions of casual leisure. This becomes a sort of antidote, promoting the sense of a permanent lack of time. Going further, note that this development is ever more consequential in our society, for there is a progressive deterioration of one of its central tools, efficient and powerful for centuries of controlling schedules as a means controlling people. A society where different cultures live legitimately side by side, where singularity is no more bizarre, where relativity systematically undermines attempts at normative regulation, a society is unable to control timetables; that is, it is unable to control its people, their identities, their reason for being.

Slowly but surely, temporal space becomes a personal issue. It is a space threatened by emptiness, open to all the opportunities and all the escapist temptations of the moneyed class, a space ready to receive all the radical ideologies of those who are thrown from the frenetic carousel of consumption. The stake is crucial, the issue imperative: are we able to manage this space, which was until now, in the hands, or more exactly, in the machinery, of the community?

Family Impact

A few days ago, a mature woman complained that the books for very young children fail to present the various types of family. Absent was her specific case, a family with one father, two mothers, four brothers and sisters living in two different apartments but in perfect harmony. This was the creative solution found by two very good friends, a married one with three children suggesting to her friend who wanted to be a mother before it is too late, to have a child with her husband and then join the whole family.

In the classroom pupils can tell about various family frames. After school some return to a classical ancient home, some go to one of their two addresses where their divorced parents live, some meet their sole parent, some have two male or female parents, and some, like the child of this woman, enjoy a more creative structure.

However, changes affect not only the components of the family but also its proceedings. One example is the disparity of the individual timetables of different members. Everyone goes out and comes back at different hours. Remember the fundamental importance of canonical and periodic meetings for the cohesion and control of a community. One of the basic pieces of this social framework was the meeting, three times a day, of the entire family around the table where every place was allocated by a clear hierarchy. The meals eaten together were not the final aim, only the medium. In modern families these meetings are increasingly rare. Some people, the forceful ones, manage to establish a meeting-meal once a week and thereby remain attentive to all threats impinging on their shared time.

A powerful enemy of the meeting-meal is the efficient devices – e.g., refrigerator for conservation, microwave for heating. It allows anyone to have a meal instantaneously at any hour, day and night, and to enjoy the unconditional company of a TV. Thus, the dining room is no more the vital and temporal regulating center of the family's rhythm. As a result, this space—the ancient agora of the traditional family—is used only for special occasions. Now, in modern apartments, you find an individual eating table, amounting to a lonely corner.

The mutation of collective time into the individual affects not only occupational and established time (e.g., work, studies, domestic obligations), but also free time where everyone now strives to be self-sufficient (exceptions include having to find a babysitter for young children). Imagine how these various types of family structures create difficulty for coordinating all the individual schedules. The family, as a microcosm, helps us analyze the deep changes in our conception of time, its distribution, its management, its control. Unaware of the processes that mold them, family members let themselves get snapped up by the centrifugal forces of personal need and attraction.

The modern family is at high risk of becoming a molecule around which atoms revolve (at the same domestic address), but which see each other only by chance and meet only to notice the gap between them. The ancient timetable regulated by tradition, which transcends individual will and desire, rebuilding continuously family texture and through it community, is now obsolete. The incapacity of most people to manage this new space means that, in this transitional phase between the era of work and that of leisure, time is left to adventitious circumstances, on one hand, and to countless entrepreneurs eager to take advantage of every amount of time and money freed from the social regulation, on the other.

The family is different. We can observe increasing variation, some of it harmonious and enriching, some of it horrid and unhealthy. The question here is whether these new frameworks will be deliberate creations realized by individuals conscious of the vital elements able to dignify life and aware of those which threaten to degrade it.

Impact on the Community

Let us compare two prophecies given over a 150-year interval:
- Condorcet (1795) wrote during the French Revolution: "the improvement of laws, public institutions thanks to the progress of science, is it not to bring closer, to identify the common interest of every person to the common interest of all? The target of the social art, is it not to eliminate this apparent opposition? And the country whose constitution and laws will fit quite exactly to reason and natural wish, is it not this in which virtue will be easier to practice, in which temptations to deviate will be rare and weak?" (author translation, p. 227)
- Tocqueville (1954, vol. 2) expressed himself, a while after the French Revolution, the Napoleon Empire, and the restorations about how the young American democracy inspired him. "The first thing that strikes the observation is an innumerable multitude of men, all equal and alike, incessantly endeavoring to procure the petty and paltry pleasures with which they glut their lives. Each of them, living apart, is as a stranger to the fate of all the rest; his

children and his private friends constitute to him the whole of mankind. As for the rest of his fellow citizens, he is close to them, but he does not see them; he touches them, but he does not feel them; he exists only in himself and for himself alone; and if his kindred still remain to him, he may be said at any rate to have lost his country." (p. 336)

Both men argue that community is the vital element of a human being's life. Yet, how can a community, "a concrete group based on solidarity and consensus transcending the written rules" (Encyclopédie Larousse), cope with the relaxation of its determinant influence upon the cyclic and formal meetings that are the essence of its vitality, that lie beyond the individual and individualist impulses?

The ringing bells, a technical and emotional reminder, signal the moment and location when and where members of the congregation see and sense each other. They are attracted, or repulsed, in the same geographical and religious space. It is their concrete space, or better, the space to which they belong even when not present. Nevertheless, these daily, solemn convocations impinge on individual schedules beyond personal will. We must remember that, for most of its members, they were part of concentric belongings, which the regular meetings had to reinforce in a regular and real communitarian experience. Relying on the community for care in the two senses of the word (care is help and also supervision), leads, however, to community domination of individuals' time in an era in which they went easily from one role to another, guided by habits and their commitment to canonical obligations.

What happened to the community when time, freed from social constraints, became the private propriety of every one? The community lost its absolute power to convoke its members and was reduced thereby to inviting them. Authoritarian convocation backed by social pressure through its members evolved into humble solicitation. With the end of convocation came the moment of seduction. Community leaders no more represent eternal truth, becoming now simple agents who know how to convince and attract, in a word, how to sell. We do know that changing eras also result from a growing, continuous exchange of goods and persons, and they force an end to monopoly.

The community at the beginning of the 21st century, like any firm wanting to be part of the market, must enter the market economy, which entails remodeling its product and polishing its image. The influence and the relative location of the institution are no longer obvious; neither is the time its potential members will spend in its various activities. Moreover, we have to be aware that social belongings are no more concentric and that offers for spending free time are numerous. Time, now a personal resource, is available individually to everyone, used according to personal choices.

In the Era of Leisure, time, individual by definition, is distributed according to the laws of supply and demand. That is, here "will" is more or less defined with reference to the "persuasive," even "manipulative," power of the agents who offer free-time choices.

Transition from Free Time to the Era of Leisure

Like a piece of Swiss cheese, people's schedules are showing more and more empty hours, while traditional social structures tend to disappear or at least no longer have decisive influence over how individuals use their time in general, and their free time in particular. One substantial consequence of these changes is the relatively new experience for most people of being in an "extra-role space." Here the acute question of personal identity emerges, which had and still has legitimacy through one's work role, not only for others, but also for oneself. We can go even further, for playing a role was the indispensable condition of one's existence. This is the meaning of the question posed even now: "What do you do?" Nobody asks: "What are you being?" or "Who are you?"

Though more and more people, suspecting that free time cannot be this empty space filled automatically by casual distractions, ask themselves who they are and what can justify not only their doing, but their overall being. Here they reach the threshold of creative leisure (Cohen-Gewerc, 2001), that is, the new Era of Leisure.

This new era is not a tremendous "time out" in the same way that centuries of struggle for freedom were not for the sake of being free "from" (Nietzsche, 1883/1970). This new Era of Leisure offers all people the opportunity to recover ownership of their personal time, that is to say their own life. In a world that has ceased being a stage and is now a kind of huge workshop, all have the prerogative and the responsibility to embark on their own inventive projects. This is the challenge not only for every individual, it is also a main new opportunity offered to our civilization.

It is unnecessary to show what we can easily observe. Our civilization "fails in its bases" (Gonzalez-Pecotche, 1963/1978) for three major reasons: men are not educated to know their inner selves; they are unaware of the powerful, active reality of the world of thought; and they are not trained to recognize universal laws and are alienated from their own inspirational spirit. Both strength and weakness are located in the mind. One needs only a single autonomous thought of jealousy well rooted in the mind to engender a plethora of wrong judgments and decisions. One needs only mental content uncontrolled by its natural owner, and that owner becomes a potential victim of every kind of manipulation. We can easily observe how those who have something to sell—ideologies, new trends, all kinds of devices—work hard to inculcate us with beliefs, prejudices, fashions, or brand names, using us as a vulgar raw material.

Adding to that the enfeeblement of the traditional community network, we can see how contemporary individuals everywhere are seduced away from the former hierarchies. Thus, today, commercial firms attract young and very young clients despite the will of parents and teachers. Global ideologies recruit activists around the world, who ignore local institutions and even governments.

In this period of transition, in entering the new Era of Leisure, major trends operate the world over, circumscribing a gigantic crossroad. Apparently, we distinguish two main directions:

- A sort of sterilized inheritance of modernism, the aim of which was essentially the instrumental organization of life; modernism with no vision and no future, dedicated to more and more comfort in the here and now. It is an approach ready to consume all our resources in its push toward escapism and casual "petty and paltry pleasures" free from any commitment to future in general and future of the humankind especially: a sort of sweet hopelessness.
- A deep wave back to the "moral" world of the past, with its clear-cut definitions and boundaries all around. Back to "our" collective "roots" and defined identity nourished with "our" beliefs and lead by "our" quasi-prophets. The vision of this fundamentalism is to restore some notion of a Golden Age in order to help the masses overcome their exclusionary feelings in a reality they have no hope of dominating

The new Era of Leisure proposes a third, serious way. Its energy comes from personal, conscious hope. A hope we can nourish with our own efforts to improve our capacity to observe and study what we experience, and to experience what we have learned. This perspective arises in the minds of those who can perceive the new horizon opened by a growing free-time space in which they can hear their aspiration for significant existence and take up the challenge to realize it. Thanks to meaningful leisure education, children will be trained to practice personal freedom "for" (Nietzsche, 1883/1970) and define their personal palette for creating their own destinies, according to their intimate commitment to sharing that part of humanity for which they are responsible.

This process is not sterile individualism (alienated addiction to ego-centric envy and temptation), but fertile individuality. Authentic uniqueness will rise not from isolation, but from open contact with the world. Leisure education can and must promote a sort of process reminiscent of the existential experience of an artist who is interested not in copying, but in creating. This is how Van Gogh found inspiration, from among others such as Jean François Millet and in Japanese prints, to realize his very special body of work, assuming full responsibility by signing his paintings.

At the twilight of the once dominant Era of Work (Stebbins, 2004), we have become conscious of being individuals, of having separate identities in this new space we call free time. Here we have an inner sense of freedom, with total accountability to ourselves. Are we up to this? Have we the necessary strength? Let us stress again two critical elements that should influence our vision for the future, especially the vision of everyone who is in a leadership position.

First, the tool of control, which had shown its efficiency for centuries, is now quite outdated, even in traditional groups. An example illustrates this new reality. Until a few years ago when a child had a phone call, it was common for a parent to answer and hear who is asking for the child. Now, aided by the cell phone, nobody knows with whom the child is talking. A teenager can easily speak, a few meters from his or her legal guardians, either with a good friend about the next examination at school, or with a drug dealer.

Second, the end has come for all sorts of monopoly. The influential, manipulative market is open, worldwide, and can directly reach nearly everyone. Governments, like parents and all authorities, have definitely lost their monopoly, and there is no way other than to delegate to children and citizens the personal responsibility for controlling themselves, hoping they can critically screen all data coming to them.

Watching our leaders at all levels, and the masses around, we must conclude that we urgently need a serious program of education, solid training, and personal empowerment.

Leisure and Empowerment

Humankind's action is moved by two main factors: needs and aspirations. Needs are closely connected with survival (i.e., to ensure life); aspirations have to do with the kind of life one wants to live. Needs and survival are the basis of life; aspirations look beyond and respond to the inner appeal for meaning. Needs mean dependence; aspirations mean invitation and free will.

Much of a person's misery has to do with the confusion between these two concepts, when more and more "needs," which have nothing to do with survival, waste almost all human time and energy. It seems that the market economy is a network driving the entire world like a motorcycle forced to go faster and faster to maintain its fragile equilibrium. The fuel for the market economy is consumption, and consumption tends to encourage more and more "needs." It is important to stress that more needs engender greater dependence. More needs to fulfill require increased energy to meet them, which in turn leaves less energy for expressing free will.

Let us apply this reasoning to free time and leisure. As they deal with their growing needs, more people have to invest a greater amount of time and energy to meet them. During this process, time, money, and energy are devoured. Every day brings a lot of "musts," such as a new distraction, or a new device that people "cannot live without." Even when people try to escape this self-defeating spiral, they often discover other needs to consume, as seen in short and miraculous "seminars" for better relationships, success in business, or the ultimate spiritual experience.

Being constantly trapped by new needs, people have no opportunity to experiment with the emergence of this inner call we label "aspiration." Two ancient terms for leisure, the Greek schole and the Roman otium, both of which could lead to self-improvement, have degenerated in modern times into words for the distractions that lead people away from themselves. Nietzsche's Zarathushtra said: "I teach you how to be superhuman. Men exist only to be outdone." (Nietzsche, 1883/1970). The famous "bread and circuses" in Rome were aimed at anesthetizing the plebs and keeping them at their low level so they could not attain the level of consciousness needed to find aspiration. With aspiration comes the attribute of life dignity.

Coming back to our global market and the needs plague, we can compare this process in its acute manifestation to the carcinogenic process when cancerous cells grow, absorbing all the energy and provoking the weakening of all the healthy organs. This procedure becomes possible because certain cells have high potentiality to become cancerous.

Promoting more and more needs among people is much the same. The countless commercial campaigns to create these new needs exploit, quite scientifically, such human weaknesses as vanity, envy, and greed. All the attention freed for investment in our inner flowering gets diverted toward consumption. Consequently the time, money, and energy freed up in this new era will become inexorably lost, should people miss the chance to learn to manage the new opportunities available there.

A popular saying states that, knowing the size of an inherited wealth, we can estimate how many generations it will take to squander it. Can we forecast how fast the opportunities of the new era will be squandered? All depends on our capacity to apprehend the transcendental potential of time, in general, and free time, in particular. This, in turn, depends on how far we can see beyond ourselves, how deep we can go with our aspirations, how determined we are to realize our commitment as human beings, inspired by dignity and sincere solidarity.

Let us remember that real free time is the privileged space freed, not only from need and obligation, but also from prejudice and taboo, which separate man from "the self." It is an extraterritorial space, where one has the opportunity to meet one's inner self, one's authentic aspirations. Only there can casual free time develop into leisure time. There, in my leisure time, I can experience the serene palpitation of my genuine being trying to express my intimate vision, trying to realize it. Here far from infantile impulse, slave of the caprices of temperament, we can concentrate all our senses on listening, with emotion, to our aspiration to be. Here arise many facets of myself that I was unaware of, since until now, no thing or person solicited them. Here I have a chance to know my entire self. This is real empowerment, that is, improvement of my being and not merely refinement of some skills to show off with.

There also resides the full enrichment of life, because leisure time is no more something apart: a sort of parenthesis, distraction, or even diversion. Conscious of the deep significance of life as a whole, we can now overcome its artificial division, imposed by religion, into holy moments and secular living, paralleled in everyday life by the discrete ideas of work time and leisure time. Having experienced the leisure state of mind, we can conceive of life as a whole, as being an entire person. Here we can sense all aspects of life, all observations, all insights felt in earlier years.

Entering this new realm of existence I feel my human unity and its two tangible components, the physical and the spiritual. I perceive this unity when I care for essential needs and maintenance of life, with the second inspiring revelation of the meaningful being I aspire to become. Gonzalez-Pecoche (1996) calls this the process of conscious self-improvement. It includes the main Socratic recommendation of knowing one's own self, which includes the essential knowledge of our three systems: instinctive, sensitive, and mental. Knowing these systems and their respective attributes entails dominating their performance to the benefit of one's free will. Then, with basic needs reasonably met, people can be receptive, meditating their connection with their spiritual inspiration and their authentic, unique being.

In entering the open space of leisure time, we enable ourselves to sense the transcendental world, even when tackling a new exercise in piano or molding a lump of clay. We achieve this sense, because in our leisure state of mind, we are not executing a simple task; rather, we are embarking on the long and exciting route toward discovery of our inner self, that part of being human that is most appealing. Thus, a budding musician discovers the supreme joy of playing an instrument, feeling how sounds emerge from his/her inner self and thereby building a bridge between him/her and him/herself. We can observe a chief executive, entirely covered with soot, sweating, working hard to curve a piece of iron and with a large smile on his lips. He feels a profound communion between the mass of material, his muscles, and his powerful aspiration to be himself. It could be also an amateur singer in a small chorale or a volunteer in a charitable organization. The common denominator is free and personal determination.

Being able to recognize such appeal, and being in a leisure mood, we should be able to see it everywhere, should we care to recognize its presence in ourselves. This requires consciousness and permanent attention. It is like the specific sound we have to distinguish during a hearing test in which more and more sounds are introduced. In encountering ourselves in the extraterritorial field of the leisure state of mind, we ought to remember that when we return from it. Having seen and recognized some of the essential qualities of what can be a significant life, we should keep in touch with this important personal discovery.

We experience the special idea of "times union" (Gonzalez-Pecotche, 1953), which means we are able to add one to another, pieces of reflection, of realization, of knowledge. That is, we are able to extract the essence of this passing hour, the essence of which goes through with us as part of our present. This is time rescued. We do feel then that the clock ticks on, but not personal time gained in realization; realization which is only the projection of its essence, the cognition which lights up my present and reveals the first signs of my future. Starting with this spiritual donation we call intuition, we do know that it's only a first step and that we are responsible for all the others to come.

Poets and composers know that the first phrase of a poem or a symphony is generally a gift. Then the mission is to engage one's efforts, and make the next lines worthy of this divine present. The inner message emerging sometimes while experiencing genuine leisure, invites the individual to respond, that is, to realize it. Realization means empowerment, process, and perseverance. One of the basic steps will resort to what Gonzalez-Pecoche (1993) calls "authority-thought" or "a thought that is instituted in the mind, by the will of the individual himself. It is responsible for giving permanency to his aspirations and purposes." (p. 48)

In experiencing leisure one discovers a very special feeling: personal existence as an absolute reality. It is independent of any role we fill; it need not be legitimated. My existence is not the result of some social need; my existence is self-sufficient. When this occurs, what strength we feel, but also what a challenge! We have overcome external dependencies, while becoming conscious of our commitment to our inner self. Being conscious of that, we can accede to the transcendental commitment of being a responsible part of humanity. Here resides the basic difference between past and present—between the past era where we were required to reproduce canonical life—and the present where we have to create from the chaos around us and in us a unique new order and the unique text of our being.

Being conscious of the great difference between need and aspiration, we gather the best of our vital energy to realize life, our life. However, "it is necessary to defeat death in order to feel and know what life really is. Death is defeated by defeating inertia, which is lack of life, and by defeating distraction, which is lack of consciousness" (Gonzalez-Pecotche, 1953, p. 115).

Transcending casual free time should be the main benefit of leisure education, which prepares us for our initiation into the domain of leisure (Spector & Cohen-Gewerc, 2001). Leisure experience offers us the opportunity to encounter our intimate resources, sense the strength of all our faculties (not just those demanded by our various roles), and initiate the long and moving dialogue between what we are and what we aspire to realize. In this process, in this vision of life, we will often fall short of our goals, but even then, we will glimpse signs of progress.

Leisure, Happiness, and Well-Being

The richest personal development can be achieved through either work or leisure. For a fortunate few, this happens in both spheres. More particularly, this state is most likely to emerge from pursuing devotee work, serious leisure, and to some extent, project-based leisure. "Devotee work" is a job that, in its appeal, resembles serious leisure, but from which the devotee gains a livelihood (Stebbins, 2006a). Happiness and well-being in devotee work and serious leisure rest on the same principles, among them, a long and profoundly rewarding career in a given work or leisure role sustained by the rewards listed in chapter 1 and the sense of self-fulfillment that comes from experiencing them.

Several of the earlier chapters describe just how this career (work or leisure) is embedded in the life course of the person, a development that can extend into old age and may start as early as adolescence. Both formal and informal education help, most significantly, in establishing this career, with leisure education being a main part of both types. To the extent that it roots in lifelong learning, self-directed learning, and adult education (where these are separate processes), leisure education fosters personal development.

At present, the impression gained from reading medical literature on health is that the term "leisure" is a dirty word. In medical literature leisure only seems to be discussed in pejorative terms; we suspect because it is regarded, not as an avenue to the Heaven of Good Health, but as a road to the Hell of Bad Health. To be sure, the common sense view of leisure's place in everyday life is partly valid. Some people do indeed smoke, eat, and drink alcohol too much; live a sedentary existence in their free time; and watch television to the point of dulling their wits; all in the name of leisure. Boredom in free time, though technically not leisure, as pointed out earlier, is nevertheless a further popular indicator of the (mentally) unhealthy lifestyle that can develop after work and other obligations have been met.

However, as we have been arguing, some leisure can also bring healthy benefits. It has been observed (Stebbins, 2006a) that, although the relationship is probably more complex than this, we may generally say that self-fulfillment, whether achieved through serious or project-based leisure or through devotee work, leads to enhanced quality of life and well-being and continues on to improved psychological health and physical health, to the extent the second is influenced by the first. It is worth noting that Damasio (2006) cautions that this well-being/health link remains hypothetical, in that evidence from controlled experimentation to support it is still lacking. So, to be more precise, the road to the Hell of Bad Health may be paved with a diet too rich in casual leisure, but the one leading to the Heaven of Good Health is paved with a judicious amount of serious leisure. We must now add in light of the serious leisure perspective, mixed with some casual or project-based leisure, if not both. In other words, to find an optimal leisure lifestyle is to get on the road to good health. Furthermore, finding and remaining in devotee work can add significantly to reaching this positive state.

All this, however, is best understood within the framework of preventive medicine. Obviously, for those people who have bad or weak physical health, an optimal leisure lifestyle alone is not going to miraculously restore them to a healthy state. For example, someone with bone cancer or another life-threatening disability could still develop an optimal leisure lifestyle, which might positively affect that person's future mental health. In the meantime, however, the patient is physically unhealthy and, so far as we know, leisure can do nothing to ameliorate the cancer. Thus, the proposition of fulfillment, quality of life, and well-being seems most applicable, most valid, in the preventive sphere of health.

Unfortunately, as a profession, preventive medicine appears to be largely unaware of this proposition. In January, 2005, Stebbins presented a seminar on it to the professors and graduate students of the, at that time, newly established Markin Institute at the University of Calgary. The Institute's mandate is to conduct research on and improve practice in preventive medicine and public health. Signs were that the talk was warmly received, in good part perhaps, because it contained ideas seen as fresh. Few, if any, of those in attendance had thought of leisure as an avenue to the Heaven of Good Health, though it was clear that they knew a great deal about leisure's other road.

That little seminar has not transformed thinking in preventive medicine (even in Calgary, as far as we can tell), nor did we realistically expect it would. In modern times, the notion of leisure as a trivial pursuit dominates, consequently leading to a great need for leisure education. Still, to be fair, a subsequent draft plan for the Markin Institute (dated February 2006) has on page 9 listed "recreation" and "neighborhood sporting clubs" among the mechanisms that lead to good health. These are not our terms, but just the same, they are welcome signs that, in the eyes of researchers at this Institute, leisure does figure in the formula for mental and, possibly, physical well-being.

On a broader plane, mental (and possibly physical) well-being hinges on having a positive state of mind. What does this mean for the fields of leisure and leisure education? Stebbins (2006c) recently concluded that, of the three forms, serious leisure is by far the most likely to generate positive psychological states. The following states—they are not presented in any particular order nor do they constitute an exhaustive list—are experienced exclusively or most deeply by participants in serious leisure. All these states are widely recognized in the field of positive psychology, where some have also received considerable empirical scrutiny. Parenthetical references refer to bibliographic sources that more directly treat the psychological state in question than done up to this point. The following list is adapted from Stebbins, 2006c:

- Self-fulfillment
- Flow
- Education (leisure education)
- Self-recognized personal strengths/resources
- Self-enrichment through a leisure experience
- Self-expression of personal strengths
- Self-actualization relative to an activity
- Personal growth in general (as seen in leisure career)
- Respectable identity (according to reference group)
- Self-esteem (as inferred from respectable identity)
- Well-being
- Resiliency (as inferred from well-being)
- Contemplation and spirituality (Stebbins, 2006b)

Conclusions

Let us conclude by observing that effort assumes two forms. There is effort put toward manipulating means and effort put toward framing goals. The experience of making these efforts, in manipulating means to reach valued ends, can be most exhilarating. It is during such experience that we come to know the inner self as it bears on the means and ends. Effort may be painful in some way, but this condition has great value, sometimes even more than the goal it helps us reach. Thanks to effort, we obtain from ourselves more than we thought we had, we grow (Bergson in Cohen-Gewerc, 1997). Leisure—and work that is like leisure—is the arena in life in which most of these formative efforts and resulting personal growth are found.

"We hold these truths to be self-evident, that all men are created equal, that they are endowed by their Creator with certain unalienable Rights, that among these are Life, Liberty and the pursuit of Happiness" (2nd paragraph in the Declaration of Independence, USA, 1776).

References

Bergson, H. (1932). *Les deux sources de la morale et de la religion.* Paris: P.U.F.

Cohen-Gewerc, E. (1997). The declining of the value "effort"; Consequences in school. In E. Paldi (Ed.), *Education and the challenge of time.* Tel Aviv: Ramot-Tel Aviv University Publisher.

Cohen-Gewerc, E. (2001). Boredom, threshold of creative leisure. *Gerontology, 30*(1-2), 87–95. Tel Aviv, Israel: Israel Gerontological Society.

Condorcet, Marquis de (1795). *Esquisse d'un tableau historique des progrès de l'esprit humain.* [Html edition for Eliohs by Guido Abbattista, February 1998]. Retrieved October 9, 2007, from http://www. eliohs.unifi.it/testi/700/condorcet/index.html

Damasio, A. (2006). *Understanding the biology of emotion.* Paper presented at the Third European Conference on Positive Psychology, University of Minho, Braga, Portugal, July.

Gonzalez-Pecotche, C. B. (1953). *Introducción al conocimiento logosófico.* Sao Paulo, Brazil: Editora Logosófica.

Gonzalez-Pecotche, C. B. (1963/1978). *Curso de iniciación logosófica.* Sao Paulo, Brazil: Editora Logosófica.

Gonzalez-Pecotche, C. B. (1993). *The spirit.* Sao Paulo, Brazil: Editora Logosófica.

Nietzsche, F. (1883/1970). *Thus spoke Zarathustra.* Tel Aviv, Israel: Shoken Publishers (in Hebrew).

Putnam, R.D. (2000). *Bowling alone: The collapse and revival of American Community.* New York: Simon & Schuster.

Rojek, C. (2002). Civil labour, leisure and post work society. *Loisir Société et/Society and Leisure, 25,* 21–36.

Spector C. and Cohen-Gewerc, E. (2001). From education to initiation, Leisure as a second chance. *World Leisure Journal, 43*(3), 48–53.

Stebbins, R. A. (2004). *Between work and leisure: The common ground of two separate worlds.* New Brunswick, NJ: Transaction.

Stebbins, R. A. (2006a). *Serious leisure: A perspective for our time.* New Brunswick, NJ: Transaction.

Stebbins, R. A. (2006b). Contemplation as leisure and nonleisure. *LSA newsletter (leisure studies association),* 73 (March), 21–23.

Stebbins, R. A. (2006c). *The serious leisure perspective and positive psychology.* Paper presented at the Third European Conference on Positive Psychology, University of Minho, Braga, Portugal, July.

Tocqueville, A. (1954). *America in democracy.* New York: Vintages Books.

Other Books by Venture Publishing, Inc.

Venture Publishing, Inc.
1999 Cato Avenue
State College, PA 16801
Phone: 814-234-4561
Fax: 814-234-1651